Jerry Kaplan is Professor Emeritus of Mathematics Education at Seton Hall University. Previously, he taught at Teachers College, Columbia University, and the University of Tel Aviv, Israel.

He is the author of mathematics books for SRA, Random House, Harcourt Brace, Triumph Learning, and School Specialty. Jerry has long advocated for combining basic skills along with challenging problems as integral parts of good math instruction.

Jerry led many workshops, seminars, and classes on how to combine problem solving with a focus on basic skills. He established the 4 to 1 system: over a period (month, semester, year), invest 4 times more time in basic skills than in problem solving.

His math books break down skills into small and simple steps that are easy to read.

Several beneficiaries of his work in these areas were the US Government Job Corps Program, the Ford Foundation, Educational Testing Service, and the Ministry of Education, Israel.

Jerry Kaplan

BASIC FRACTIONS

AUSTIN MACAULEY PUBLISHERS™
LONDON * CAMBRIDGE * NEW YORK * SHARJAH

Copyright © Jerry Kaplan 2024

All rights reserved. No part of this publication may be reproduced, distributed, or transmitted in any form or by any means, including photocopying, recording, or other electronic or mechanical methods, without the prior written permission of the publisher, except in the case of brief quotations embodied in critical reviews and certain other non-commercial uses permitted by copyright law. For permission requests, write to the publisher.

Any person who commits any unauthorized act in relation to this publication may be liable to criminal prosecution and civil claims for damages.

The contents of this work, including, but not limited to, the accuracy of events, people, and places depicted; opinions expressed; permission to used previously published materials included; and any advice given or actions advocated are solely the responsibility of the author, who assumes all liability for said work and indemnifies the publisher against any claims stemming from publication of the work.

This book follows the fair-use quotation guidelines for scholarly works of copy-righted material cited herein as outlined online at https://nrsvbibles.org/index.php/licensing/.

Unless otherwise stated, the default Biblical quotations cited herein are taken from the **New Revised Standard Version** of the Bible, copyright © 1989, Division of Christian Education of the National Council of Churches of Christ in the United States of America and follows the guidelines set forth online at https://nrsvbibles.org/index.php/licensing/. All rights reserved. Other versions cited are fully identified.

Ordering Information
Quantity sales: Special discounts are available on quantity purchases by corporations, associations, and others. For details, contact the publisher at the address below.

Publisher's Cataloging-in-Publication data
Kaplan, Jerry
Basic Fractions

ISBN 9798889102588 (Paperback)
ISBN 9798889102595 (Hardback)

Library of Congress Control Number: 2023924614

www.austinmacauley.com/us

First Published 2024
Austin Macauley Publishers LLC
40 Wall Street, 33rd Floor, Suite 3302
New York, NY 10005
USA

mail-usa@austinmacauley.com
+1 (646) 5125767

We owe a big thank you to Mike Neibart, middle school math teacher, who conducted major field testing in his school: Emolier Academy, Bronx, NY.

Mike and his students offered constructive commentary during the development phase of this project.

Table of Contents

Introduction 9

Chapter 1: **Introducing Fractions**

1.1 A Fraction Shows Part of a Whole 10

1.2 A Fraction Shows Part of a Group...14

1.3 Comparing Fractions with the Same Denominators...........................17

1.4 Comparing Fractions with the Same Numerators 20

1.5 Review...23

Chapter 2: **Simplifying Fractions**

2.1 Equal Fractions 25

2.2 Dividing by 2, 3, 5, 9, 10 28

2.3 Equivalent Fractions—Part 1 32

2.4 Equivalent Fractions—Part 2 37

2.5 Simplifying Fractions 40

2.6 Greatest Common Factor (GCF) 43

2.7 Two Ways of Simplifying Fractions 46

2.8 Review 50

Chapter 3: **Mixed Numbers**

3.1 Fractions Less Than, Equal To, and Greater Than 1 53

3.2 Identifying Mixed Numbers..57

3.3 Changing Improper Fractions Greater Than 1 to Mixed Numbers 60

3.4 Rounding Mixed Numbers 64

3.5 Review 68

Chapter 4: **Least Common Denominator**

4.1 Multiples 71

4.2 Using Multiples to Find a Common Denominator 74

4.3 Least Common Multiple (LCM)...78

4.4 Least Common Denominator (LCD) 81

4.5 Review 86

Chapter 5: **Comparing Fractions**

    5.1 Comparing Fractions 88

    5.2 Finding the LCD: More Than Two Fractions
        (One Denominator is a Multiple of One of the Others) 93

    5.3 Ordering Fractions *(More Than Two Fractions)* 97

    5.4 Comparing and Ordering Mixed Numbers 102

    5.5 Review 105

Chapter 6: **Adding Fractions**

    6.1 Estimating Sums and Differences 107

    6.2 Adding Fractions with Like Denominators 110

    6.3 Adding Fractions with Unlike Denominators 113

    6.4 Adding Mixed Numbers 117

    6.5 Review 121

Chapter 7: **Subtracting Fractions**

    7.1 Subtracting Fractions with Like Denominators 123

    7.2 Subtracting Fractions with Unlike Denominators 126

    7.3 Subtracting Mixed Numbers with Unlike Denominators 131

    7.4 Review 136

Chapter 8: **Multiplying Fractions**

    8.1 The Fractional Part of a Number 138

    8.2 Multiplying a Whole Number by a Fraction 142

    8.3 Multiplying Two Fractions 146

    8.4 Writing Mixed Numbers as Fractions Greater Than 1 150

    8.5 Multiplying by a Mixed Number 154

    8.6 Simplifying Before Multiplying 158

    8.7 Review 163

Chapter 9: **Dividing Fractions**

    9.1 Dividing a Whole Number by a Fraction 165

    9.2 Dividing a Fraction by Fraction or a Whole Number 169

    9.3 Dividing by a Mixed Number 173

    9.4 Review 178

Introduction

To the Student

This book, **Basic Fractions,** gives you a chance to learn about a math subject that many people think is hard and confusing. Maybe you are one of these people. If you are, we hope you will feel differently at the end of the book.

The reasons are simple. In this book, you will find that all the important skills in using fractions are broken down into small, easy-to-understand steps. You will find that each lesson is part of something bigger, and that each lesson is clear and understandable. As you master each lesson, you will feel more and more successful and you will very quickly be able to do all the skills in the book. The language is simple. The directions are clear. The entire book is designed to link your learning from one skill to the next.

Each lesson deals with a single skill. It starts with a real-life example of how the skill is used. It then gives you one or two simple rules plus several more examples to illustrate how to use the rules are used. Finally, there is an exercise section for you to practice the skill.

Some of the special things about this book are in the exercise section. There are two parts: **Exercises with Hints** and **Exercises on Your Own.** The questions of the first part come with hints that guide you in solving the problems. This helps you get ready to do the problems _without_ hints in the second section. As in the rest of the lesson, everything is done in steps, slowly and carefully. You will also find that the word problems at the end of the exercises are good examples of where and how fractions are used.

Good luck with **Basic Fractions**.

1. Introducing Fractions

1.1 A Fraction Shows Part of a Whole

You use fractions all the time. For example, you are using the fraction $\frac{1}{2}$ (one half) when you say that something costs half a dollar.

In this lesson, you will learn the names of the parts of a fraction. You will also learn how fractions are used to show a part of a whole—the way a half dollar is part of a whole dollar.

Hank looks at his computer screen. It is divided into three equal-size columns. Two of the columns are full of names. One column is full of numbers.

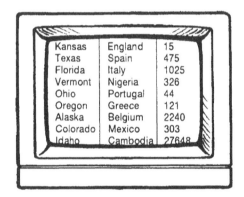

What fraction of the whole screen is used for **numbers**?

$$\frac{1}{3} = \frac{\text{number of columns with numbers}}{\text{total number of equal-size columns}}$$

So the fraction $\frac{1}{3}$ shows what fraction of the whole screen is for numbers. (We say "one third" for $\frac{1}{3}$.)

Notice that in this example, the fraction is used to show part of a whole.

Look at the computer screen again. 2 out of 3 equal columns are for names.

Which fraction of the whole screen is used for **names**?

$$\frac{1}{3} \qquad \frac{2}{3} \qquad \frac{3}{2}$$

The correct answer is $\frac{2}{3}$. Again, the fraction shows parts of a whole.

The parts of a fraction have special names:

$\frac{1}{3}$ — *numerator* (top number of the fraction)
— *fraction bar* (the line between the top and bottom numbers)
— *denominator* (bottom number of the fraction)

Remember these names! They are used all through this book, so you have to know them.

EXAMPLE 1

3 of **4** equal parts are shaded.

$\frac{3}{4}$ of the circle is shaded.

(Three fourths is shaded.)

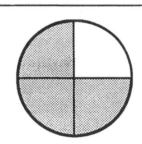

EXAMPLE 2

The parts of the rectangle are *not* all equal parts.

So we *cannot* write a fraction for the shaded parts.

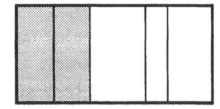

EXAMPLE 3

The 5 parts are all equal parts.

So we *can* write a fraction.

$\frac{3}{5}$ of the rectangle is shaded.

(Three fifths is shaded.)

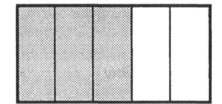

Exercises with Hints

For which of these can we write fractions? Put a check mark (✔) in front of them. *(Hint: Which of the figures are divided into equal parts?)*

1.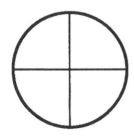

2.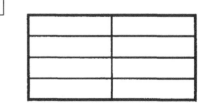

3.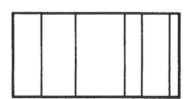

11

Use the circle below to answer Exercises 4-7.

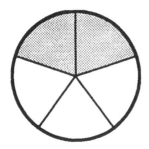

4. How many parts is the circle divided into? (Hint: Count the parts)

   _____

5. Are the parts equal?
   (Hint: Just take a good look)

   _____

6. How many parts are shaded?
   (Hint: Count the shaded parts)

   _____

7. What fraction of the circle is shaded?
   (Hint: **Numerator** = number of parts shaded. **Denominator** = total number of parts in the figure.)

   _____

Write the fraction for the shaded part of each figure that follows.

8. (Hint: **Denominator** = number of equal parts)

   _____

   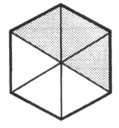

9. (Hint: **Numerator** = number of parts shaded)

   _____

   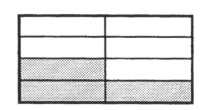

10. (Hint: Count the equal parts. Then count the parts that are shaded.)

    _____

    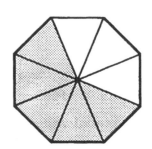

Solve.

11. Chun is a designer of special mailings for his company. He is working on a brochure that is divided into 3 equal parts. He will color 2 of these parts purple. What fraction of the brochure will be purple? (Hint: Remember—the number of equal parts is the **denominator**.)

    _____

Exercises on Your Own

Write a fraction for each set of words.

1. three fifths _____

2. five eighths _____

3. six tenths _____

4. two sixths _____

Write a fraction for the shaded part of each figure.

5. _____

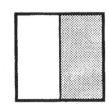

6. _____

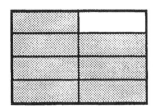

7. _____

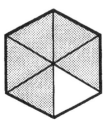

Shade each diagram to show the fraction.

8. $\frac{2}{3}$

9. $\frac{4}{5}$

10. $\frac{6}{8}$

Solve.

11. Saretha folded a sheet of paper into 4 equal parts. She wrote notes on 2 parts.

    a. What fraction of the sheet did she write on?

    _____

    b. What fraction of the sheet did she not write on?

    _____

12. Juan bought a pizza with 8 slices. He ate 3 slices. What fraction of the pizza did he eat?

    _____

13. A football field is divided into 10 equal parts. 3 parts are covered by canvas. What fraction is covered with canvas?

    _____

1.2 A Fraction Shows Part of a Group

In the last lesson, you saw how fractions were used to show parts of a whole. In this lesson, you will see another use for fractions—to show part of a group.

There are 8 people in Leroy's photography group. 3 people in the group own their own cameras.

What fraction of the group owns cameras?

- First, how many people own cameras? 3.
- Second, how many people are in the group? 8.
- 3 of the 8 people own cameras.

$$\frac{3}{8} = \frac{\text{number of people who own cameras}}{\text{number of people in group}}$$

$\frac{3}{8}$ of the people own cameras.

In this example, the fraction is used to show part of a group.

What fraction of the people do *not* own cameras?

$$\frac{3}{5} \qquad \frac{3}{8} \qquad \frac{8}{3} \qquad \frac{5}{8}$$

- First, figure out how many of the 8 people do not own cameras.
- If 3 people do own cameras, then 5 do not. (8 − 3 = 5)

Now you can write the fraction of the people that do not own cameras.

The correct answer is $\frac{5}{8}$.

Again, the fraction shows part of a group.

1.2 A FRACTION SHOWS PART OF A GROUP

> **EXAMPLES**
>
> **6** of a team of **9** baseball players are left handed.
>
> $\frac{6}{9}$ of the players are left handed.
>
> **2** of **7** pieces of candy are red.
>
> $\frac{2}{7}$ of the pieces of candy are red.
>
> **15** of the **25** people in Peggy's department voted for a new recycling procedure.
>
> $\frac{15}{25}$ of Peggy's department voted for recycling.

Exercises with Hints

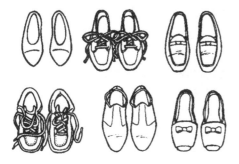

1. How many shoes are there altogether? _____

2. How many shoes have laces? _____

3. Write a fraction for the shoes with laces. (*Hint: the denominator is the **total** number of shoes. The numerator is the number of shoes **with laces.***)

   _____

Study the next drawing. Then answer questions 4-6.

4. How many forks and spoons are there? _____

5. How many forks are there? _____

6. Write a fraction for the number of forks. (*Hint: the denominator is the **total** number of forks and spoons. The numerator is the number of forks.*)

   _____

7. How many O's are in the word **MICROPROCESSOR**?

   _____

8. How many letters are in the word **MICROPROCESSOR** altogether?

   _____

9. What fraction of the letters in **MICROPROCESSOR** are O's? (*Hint: Be careful! Which number is the denominator? Which is the numerator?*)

   _____

Solve.

10. Sophia is taking an accounting course on Tuesday evenings. She is the only female in her class of 12 students.

    a. What fraction of the class is female? *(Hint: Is 12 the numerator or denominator?)*

    _____

    b. What fraction of the class is male? *(Hint: How many males are there in the class?)*

    _____

Exercises on Your Own

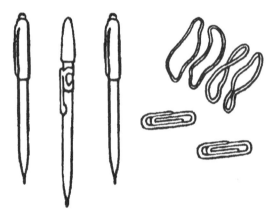

1. What fraction of these things are pens? _____

2. What fraction of the figures above are circles? _____

Solve.

3. It rained 3 days of the week last week. What fraction of the week did it rain?

   _____

4. Rosa works with 8 other people. She is the only one who walks to work. What fraction of the group walks to work?

   _____

5. Joe has 6 pennies, 4 nickels, and 5 dimes.

   a. What fraction of the coins are pennies? _____

   b. What fraction are nickels? _____

   c. What fraction are dimes? _____

6. Three of Felix's 7 computer disks are filled with data. The others have no data on them.

   a. What fraction of the disks are filled with data?

   _____

   b. What fraction of the disks have nothing on them?

   _____

1.3 Comparing Fractions with the Same Denominators

You can compare fractions to see which is larger or smaller. But you can only do this easily if they have the _same numerator or the same denominator._

This lesson shows you how to compare fractions with the same denominator.

- -

Toshiro and Kate are using ribbons to wrap packages.

Toshiro has a ribbon that is $\frac{5}{8}$ meter long. Kate has a ribbon $\frac{4}{8}$ meters long. Which ribbon is longer?

- $\frac{5}{8}$ means **5** of 8 equal parts.

- $\frac{4}{8}$ means **4** of 8 equal parts.

- 5 parts are more than 4 parts. So, $\frac{5}{8}$ is greater than $\frac{4}{8}$.

Toshiro's ribbon is longer.

- -

The symbols **>** and **<** are often used to compare numbers.

The symbol **>** means **"is greater than."**

$\frac{5}{8}$ > $\frac{4}{8}$ (That is, $\frac{5}{8}$ **is greater than** $\frac{4}{8}$)

The symbol **<** means **"is less than."**

$\frac{4}{8}$ < $\frac{5}{8}$ (That is, $\frac{4}{8}$ **is less than** $\frac{5}{8}$)

REMEMBER:

Here's a way to remember the difference between the symbols **>** and **<**.

- The symbol **>** has the **greater** (larger) **end first**. It means **"is greater than."**
- The symbol **<** has the **lesser** (smaller) **end first**. It means **"is less than."**

- -

RULE _for comparing fractions with the same denominator:_

> _If two fractions have the same denominator (it's called a <u>common denominator</u>), then the fraction with the <u>greater numerator</u> is the greater fraction._

But remember—the fractions must have a _common denominator_ for this rule to work!

1. INTRODUCING FRACTIONS

SPECIAL NOTE:

The word **common** has a special meaning in math. It means "alike," or "similar," or "the same." We use this meaning in everyday language when we say that two people have many things **in common**. This means that they are alike, or similar.

So when we say that two fractions have a *common* denominator, we mean that they have *the same* denominator—a denominator *in common.*

EXAMPLE 1

Maria needs $\frac{3}{4}$ cup of sugar and $\frac{2}{4}$ cup of flour.

Does she need more sugar or flour?

The fractions $\frac{3}{4}$ and $\frac{2}{4}$ have a common denominator—4.

So you can compare the numerators:

$3 > 2$. (3 is greater than 2)

So $\frac{\mathbf{3}}{\mathbf{4}} > \frac{\mathbf{2}}{\mathbf{4}}$. Maria needs more sugar.

EXAMPLE 2

$\frac{5}{12}$ of a group of pens are red. $\frac{3}{12}$ of the pens are blue.

Are there more red pens or blue pens?

$\frac{5}{12}$ and $\frac{3}{12}$ have the same denominator—12.

So you can compare the numerators:

$5 > 3$.

So $\frac{5}{12} > \frac{3}{12}$. There are more red pens.

Exercises with Hints

Check (✔) the pairs of fractions that have a common denominator. *(Hint: Remember that the denominator is the number below the fraction bar. Second hint: A **common denominator** is the same denominator for both fractions.)*

1. ☐ $\frac{5}{7}$ $\frac{4}{7}$

2. ☐ $\frac{2}{21}$ $\frac{21}{22}$

3. ☐ $\frac{4}{5}$ $\frac{1}{5}$

1.3 COMPARING FRACTIONS WITH THE SAME DENOMINATORS

Look at the pairs of diagrams. Each pair shows 2 fractions. Write > or < in the blank. Be careful—be sure you know the difference between the two signs!

4. $\frac{5}{7}$ ___ $\frac{3}{7}$

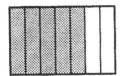 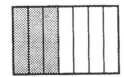

5. $\frac{5}{6}$ ___ $\frac{4}{6}$

6. $\frac{4}{8}$ ___ $\frac{6}{8}$

Solve.

7. Ramona and Tom work in the same bakery. Ramona works $\frac{2}{5}$ of a full week and Tom works $\frac{4}{5}$ of a full week. Who works more, Ramona or Tom?
(Hint: Compare numerators.)

Exercises on Your Own

Write < or > in the blanks.

1. $\frac{2}{3}$ ___ $\frac{1}{3}$
2. $\frac{5}{9}$ ___ $\frac{7}{9}$
3. $\frac{8}{13}$ ___ $\frac{7}{13}$
4. $\frac{5}{10}$ ___ $\frac{8}{10}$
5. $\frac{7}{13}$ ___ $\frac{5}{13}$
6. $\frac{1}{7}$ ___ $\frac{6}{7}$
7. $\frac{2}{50}$ ___ $\frac{45}{50}$
8. $\frac{4}{5}$ ___ $\frac{1}{5}$

Solve.

9. Julie read $\frac{9}{24}$ of a book about animals. Doris read $\frac{5}{24}$ of the same book. Who read more, Julie or Doris? _____

10. Willie mowed $\frac{3}{8}$ of his lawn. His brother Bart mowed $\frac{5}{8}$ of the same lawn. Who mowed more of the lawn?

11. Nuna is the manager of a theater. She said that the theater was $\frac{1}{4}$ full on Friday and $\frac{3}{4}$ full on Saturday. On which night were there more people?

12. Cesar looked at a list of union members. He said that $\frac{3}{8}$ of the people on the list had not had eye exams, and that $\frac{1}{8}$ had not paid their dues. Which group was larger—people who did not have eye exams or people who did not pay their dues?

1.4 Comparing Fractions with the Same Numerators

In the last lesson, you learned how to compare fractions that have a common *denominator*. Now you will learn how to compare fractions that have the same *numerator*.

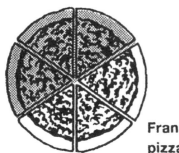
Frank's pizza

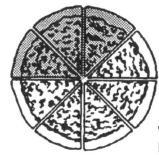
Jodie's pizza

Pizzas at the mall are all the same size, but they are cut into either 6 or 8 slices.

Frank ate $\frac{3}{6}$ of a pizza and Jodie ate $\frac{3}{8}$ of a pizza.

Who ate more pizza, Frank or Jodie?

- Frank and Jodie ate the same number of slices.
- But each of Frank's slices is bigger.

So, Frank ate more pizza.

You have just compared fractions with the same numerators, but *different* denominators.

Here is another way to compare fractions with the same numerators—by comparing diagrams.

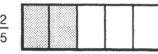
$\frac{2}{5}$

$\frac{2}{7}$

Which is greater, $\frac{2}{5}$ or $\frac{2}{7}$?

The diagrams show that $\frac{2}{5} > \frac{2}{7}$ ($\frac{2}{5}$ is greater than $\frac{2}{7}$)

RULE for comparing fraction with the same numerators:

> If two fractions have the same numerator, then the fraction with the <u>smaller denominator</u> is the greater fraction.

1.4 COMPARING FRACTIONS WITH THE SAME NUMERATORS

If you don't understand why this rule is true, look back at the diagrams in this chapter.

EXAMPLE

$\frac{7}{8}$ and $\frac{7}{12}$ have the same numerator.

Compare the denominators:

$\qquad 8 < 12.$

So $\frac{7}{8}$ is the fraction with the smaller denominator.

Therefore, $\frac{7}{8} > \frac{7}{12}$ ($\frac{7}{8}$ is greater than $\frac{7}{12}$).

Exercises with Hints

1. The rule for comparing two fractions with the **same numerator** states that the fraction with the smaller denominator is the—

   a. greater fraction

   b. smaller fraction

2. The rule for comparing two fractions with the **same denominator** (see *Lesson 1.3*) states that the fraction with the greater numerator is the—

   a. greater fraction

   b. smaller fraction

Which pairs of fractions have the same **numerators**?
(Hint: The numerator is the number above the fraction bar.)

3. $\frac{9}{13}$, $\frac{9}{15}$

4. $\frac{1}{6}$, $\frac{6}{23}$

5. $\frac{4}{13}$, $\frac{1}{13}$

6. $\frac{12}{17}$, $\frac{12}{13}$

Which pair of fractions have the same **denominators**?
(Hint: The denominator is the number below the fraction bar.)

7. $\frac{2}{14}$, $\frac{14}{15}$

8. $\frac{7}{8}$, $\frac{1}{8}$

9. $\frac{9}{10}$, $\frac{10}{10}$

10. $\frac{5}{6}$, $\frac{6}{7}$

In each pair, circle the fraction that is smaller.
(Hint: Look back at the rule if you need to.)

11. $\frac{2}{3}$ or $\frac{2}{9}$

12. $\frac{5}{6}$ or $\frac{5}{12}$

13. $\frac{1}{20}$ or $\frac{1}{2}$

I. INTRODUCING FRACTIONS

In each pair, circle the fraction that is smaller. *(Hint: In some pairs, the denominators are the same. In some pairs, the numerators are the same. Be careful! Look back at the rules in the last lesson and in this lesson if you need to.)*

14. $\frac{4}{5}$ or $\frac{4}{7}$

15. $\frac{3}{5}$ or $\frac{4}{5}$

16. $\frac{7}{8}$ or $\frac{3}{8}$

17. $\frac{2}{7}$ or $\frac{2}{3}$

Solve.

18. Rudy spends $\frac{2}{5}$ of her work day at a computer and another $\frac{2}{7}$ talking on the telephone. What does he spend more time doing?
(Hint: Which fraction has the smaller denominator?)

   a. working at a computer

   b. talking on the phone

Exercises on Your Own

In each pair, draw a circle around the fraction that is **greater**.

1. $\frac{3}{10}$ or $\frac{9}{10}$

2. $\frac{9}{11}$ or $\frac{9}{100}$

3. $\frac{1}{7}$ or $\frac{1}{3}$

4. $\frac{2}{5}$ or $\frac{4}{5}$

In each pair, draw a circle around the fraction that is **smaller**.

5. $\frac{6}{15}$ or $\frac{6}{7}$

6. $\frac{3}{30}$ or $\frac{3}{4}$

7. $\frac{5}{8}$ or $\frac{1}{8}$

8. $\frac{9}{11}$ or $\frac{9}{25}$

Write **<** or **>** in the blanks.

9. $\frac{7}{14}$ —— $\frac{7}{19}$

10. $\frac{9}{10}$ —— $\frac{1}{10}$

11. $\frac{2}{13}$ —— $\frac{2}{4}$

Solve.

12. Serena brought $\frac{3}{8}$ of the total number of cookies for the meeting tonight. Raheem brought $\frac{3}{12}$ of the cookies for tonight. Who brought more, Serena or Raheem?

_____

13. Ramon painted $\frac{5}{9}$ of a wall. Karen painted another $\frac{5}{6}$ of the same wall. Who painted more of the wall, Ramon or Karen?

_____

14. Sally spent $\frac{1}{3}$ of her lunch hour at the bank and $\frac{1}{4}$ eating. Which took longer?

   a. going to the bank

   b. eating

1.5 Review

Write a fraction for the shaded part of each.

1. _____

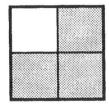

2. _____

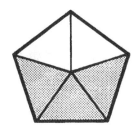

3. _____

Write a fraction for each set of words.

4. nine tenths _____

5. four sixths _____

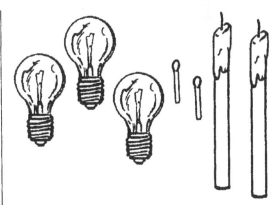

6. What fraction of these things are light bulbs? _____

7. What fraction of these things are cups? _____

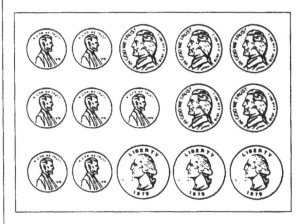

8. What fractions of these coins are nickels? _____

1. INTRODUCING FRACTIONS

Write **<** or **>** in the blanks.

9. $\dfrac{4}{5}$ —— $\dfrac{2}{5}$

10. $\dfrac{7}{11}$ —— $\dfrac{6}{11}$

11. $\dfrac{6}{13}$ —— $\dfrac{5}{13}$

12. $\dfrac{2}{7}$ —— $\dfrac{2}{9}$

13. $\dfrac{3}{10}$ —— $\dfrac{3}{14}$

14. $\dfrac{7}{25}$ —— $\dfrac{7}{20}$

Solve.

15. Ramona spoke for $\dfrac{5}{6}$ of an hour. Julia spoke for $\dfrac{5}{8}$ of an hour. Who spoke longer, Ramona or Julia?

————————

16. Donna walks $\dfrac{3}{10}$ of a mile to her job. Karl walks $\dfrac{7}{10}$ of a mile to his job. Who has a longer walk to work, Donna or Karl?

————————

17. Freddie's resume takes up $\dfrac{3}{4}$ of a page. George's is $\dfrac{3}{5}$ of a page long. Whose resume is longer, Freddie's or George's?

————————

2. Simplifying Fractions

2.1 Equal Fractions

When you do math with fractions, you often have to work with fractions that are equal to each other. This lesson will show you what we mean by "equal fractions."

All pizzas at the Pizza Shop are cut into 8 slices.

Tammy says she wants 4 slices, or $\frac{4}{8}$ of a pizza. Marty says that Tammy wants $\frac{1}{2}$ of a pizza.

Who is right?

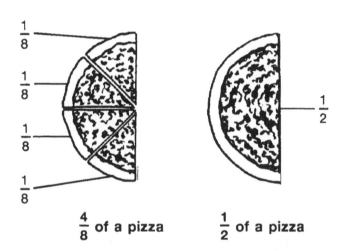

- $\frac{4}{8}$ of a pizza is the same amount as $\frac{1}{2}$ of a pizza.
- So, Tammy and Marty are both right. The fractions are equal to each other.
- $\frac{4}{8} = \frac{1}{2}$

EXAMPLE 1

$\frac{1}{4} = \frac{2}{8}$

25

2. SIMPLIFYING FRACTIONS

EXAMPLE 2

$\frac{4}{6} = \frac{2}{3}$

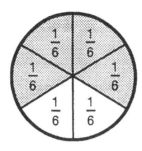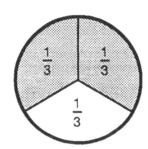

Exercises with Hints

Below each diagram, write the fraction that shows how much of each figure is shaded. *(Hint: Ask yourself: How many parts are there altogether? How many parts are shaded?)*

1. _____

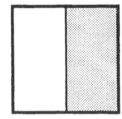

2. _____

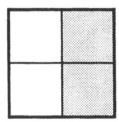

3. Fill in the missing number in the second fraction. *(Hint: Use the two squares above to find equal fractions)*

    $\frac{1}{2} = \frac{}{4}$

Use the fraction strips to find the missing numerator. Write the missing numerator in each fraction.

4. $\frac{3}{4} = \frac{}{8}$

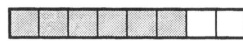

5. $\frac{6}{10} = \frac{}{5}$

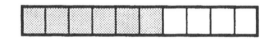

6. $\frac{2}{6} = \frac{}{3}$

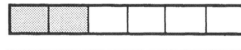

26

Exercises on Your Own

Write the missing numerators. Use the diagrams to help you.

1. $\frac{2}{10} = \frac{\ }{5}$

2. $\frac{4}{6} = \frac{\ }{3}$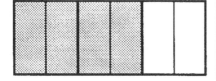

3. $\frac{4}{8} = \frac{\ }{2}$

Write the missing numerators. If you wish, shade the rectangles to help find the missing part:

4. $\frac{2}{4} = \frac{\ }{2}$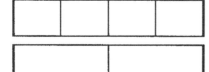

5. $\frac{1}{2} = \frac{\ }{6}$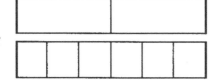

6. $\frac{1}{4} = \frac{\ }{8}$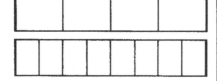

7. $\frac{2}{10} = \frac{\ }{5}$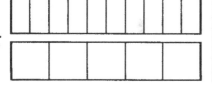

Solve.

8.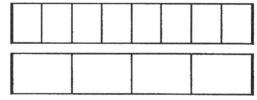

Billie weighs a bag of sugar on a scale. It weighs $\frac{6}{8}$ of a pound. Write the fraction as a fraction in fourths.

$\frac{6}{8} = \frac{\ }{4}$

9.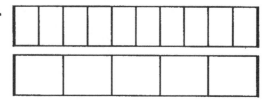

Shawanda said that $\frac{8}{10}$ of the people who work in her office wear glasses. Write the fraction $\frac{8}{10}$ in fifths.

$\frac{8}{10} = \frac{\ }{5}$

10.

Miguel cut an apple pie into 6 equal pieces, and ate 2 pieces. Complete these fractions for the part that Miguel ate:

$\frac{\ }{6}$ or $\frac{\ }{3}$

2.2 Dividing by 2, 3, 5, 9, 10

When you do math with fractions, you often have to change a fraction into another fraction that is equal to it. Before you learn how to do this, however, you have to learn a few special rules about division. They are called **divisibility rules**.

This lesson is about these divisibility rules. In the next lesson, you will learn how to use them to make equal fractions.

Molly delivers newspapers. This morning she has 135 papers. She wants to put them into equal bundles of 5 papers each.

Can Molly divide 135 papers evenly into bundles of 5?

$$\begin{array}{r} 27 \\ 5\overline{)135} \\ -10 \\ \hline 35 \\ -35 \\ \hline 0 \end{array}$$

Divide **135** by **5**:

5 divides 135 evenly, since the remainder is 0.

Molly can divide newspapers into bundles of 5.

We say 135 is **divisible by 5**, since 5 divides 135 evenly. (The word **divisible** means "can be divided." Remember this word!)

Here is a super-fast way to tell if a number is divisible (can be divided) by 5:

> **A number is divisible by 5 if the number ends in 0 or 5.**

EXAMPLES

These numbers are divisible by 5:		These numbers are *not* divisible by 5:	
490	(number ends in 0)	93	(number does *not* end in 0 or 5)
75	(number ends in 5)	507	(number does *not* end in 0 or 5)
800	(number ends in 0)	1,946	(number does *not* end in 0 or 5)
47,625	(number ends in 5)	555,001	(number does *not* end in 0 or 5)

Here are divisibility rules for the numbers 2, 3, 5, 9, and 10. These divisibility rules are important. Memorize them! You will use them over and over again in this chapter and in the chapters that follow.

You can test if a number is divisible by 2, 3, 5, 9, and 10 without having to do the division to find out. This chart will show you how.

DIVISIBILITY RULES:

A NUMBER IS DIVISIBLE BY—	IF—
2	—the number ends in 0, 2, 4, 6, or 8 (That is, it is an even number)
3	—the sum of the digits is divisible by 3
5	—the number ends in 0 or 5
9	—the sum of the digits is divisible by 9
10	—the number ends in 0

EXAMPLES

Here are examples of how all the divisibility rules work.

- *3,578, 14,* and *530* are all *divisible by 2* since they are all even numbers. The numbers end in 8, 4, and 0.
- *45* is *divisible by 3* since the sum of the digits is 4 + 5 = 9, and 9 is divisible by 3.
- *45* is also *divisible by 5* since it ends in the number 5. The number 40 is also divisible by 5, since it ends in 0.
- *2,691* is *divisible by 9* because the sum of the digits is 2 + 6 + 9 + 1 = 18, and 18 is divisible by 9.
- *780* is *divisible by 10* since it ends in 0.

If you still have trouble with these divisibilty rules, ask your teacher for help.

2. SIMPLIFYING FRACTIONS

Exercises with Hints

Use the rules in the table to answer these questions.

Put a check mark (✔) before the numbers that are divisible by **3**. *(Hint: Add the digits of each number. Is the sum divisible by 3?)*

1. ☐ 37
2. ☐ 64
3. ☐ 123
4. ☐ 678
5. ☐ 1,507
6. ☐ 9,100

Put a check mark before the numbers that are divisible by **9**. *(Hint: Add the digits of the number. Is the sum divisible by 9?)*

7. ☐ 47
8. ☐ 94
9. ☐ 576
10. ☐ 666
11. ☐ 2,873
12. ☐ 90,918

Put a check mark before the numbers that are divisible by **5**. *(Hint: Does the number end in a 5 or a 0?)*

13. ☐ 70
14. ☐ 195
15. ☐ 309
16. ☐ 455
17. ☐ 1,003
18. ☐ 75,551

Put a check mark before the numbers that are divisible by **10**. *(Hint: Does the number end in a 0?)*

19. ☐ 340
20. ☐ 255
21. ☐ 70
22. ☐ 92
23. ☐ 2,301
24. ☐ 105

Put a check mark before the numbers that are divisible by **2**. *(Hint: Does the number end in 0, 2, 4, 6, or 8?)*

25. ☐ 75
26. ☐ 76
27. ☐ 77
28. ☐ 400
29. ☐ 981
30. ☐ 465

Solve.

31. Linda works in a stationery store. The store has 243 loose pens. Can Linda divide these into—

    a) groups of 3? ___ yes ___ no

    b) groups of 5? ___ yes ___ no

    c) groups of 9? ___ yes ___ no

    (Hint: Use the Examples and Rules on page 25 to help you.)

2.2 DIVIDING BY 2, 3, 5, 9, 10

Exercises on Your Own

Put a check mark (✔) before the numbers that are divisible by **5**.

1. ☐ 503
2. ☐ 4,760
3. ☐ 875
4. ☐ 600
5. ☐ 65
6. ☐ 53

Put a check mark before the numbers that are divisible by **3**.

7. ☐ 33
8. ☐ 42
9. ☐ 61
10. ☐ 362
11. ☐ 72
12. ☐ 555

Put a check mark before the numbers that are divisible by **2**.

13. ☐ 456
14. ☐ 60
15. ☐ 75
16. ☐ 459
17. ☐ 27
18. ☐ 24

Put a check mark before the numbers that are divisible by **10**.

19. ☐ 230
20. ☐ 145
21. ☐ 20

22. ☐ 701
23. ☐ 1,000
24. ☐ 435

Put a check mark before the numbers that are divisible by **9**.

25. ☐ 81
26. ☐ 109
27. ☐ 450
28. ☐ 9,000
29. ☐ 936
30. ☐ 138

Solve.

31. John has 90 magazines that he wants to divide into equal groups. Can he divide the books into—

    a) 2 equal groups?
    ___ yes ___ no

    b) 3 equal groups?
    ___ yes ___ no

    c) 5 equal groups?
    ___ yes ___ no

    d) 9 equal groups?
    ___ yes ___ no

    e) 10 equal groups?
    ___ yes ___ no

32. Hana wants to mail 505 catalogs to special customers of her company. Can she bundle the catalogs into—

    a) groups of 5, with none left over?
    ___ yes ___ no

    b) groups of 10, with none left over?
    ___ yes ___ no

2.3 Equivalent Fractions—Part 1

There are two ways to change a fraction into another fraction that is equal to it. You can multiply. Or you can divide, using the divisibility rules you learned in the last lesson. This chapter will give you practice in doing both.

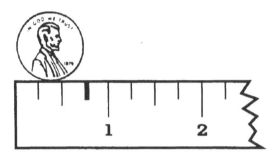

When Bob measured a penny, he found that it is $\frac{3}{4}$ inch long.

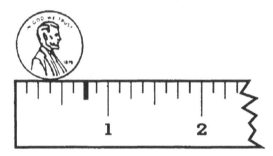

When Fran measured a penny, she found that it measured $\frac{6}{8}$ inch.

Who is right, Bob or Fran?
- Line up the rulers next to each other.

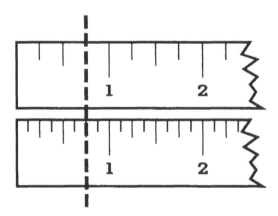

- They are both right.
- Two fractions that are equal, like $\frac{3}{4}$ and $\frac{6}{8}$, are called **equivalent fractions.**

Remember this term! You'll see it a lot.

2.3 EQUIVALENT FRACTIONS—PART 1

Here's how to find two equivalent fractions. Start with any fraction. (In math, the fraction you start with is called the *given* fraction.) Then use the methods below to find other fractions that are equivalent to the given fraction:

METHOD 1: *Making equivalent fractions by multiplying:*

> ***Multiply** the numerator and denominator of the given fraction by the same number.*

(You can always use this method.)

$$\frac{1}{2} \xrightarrow{\times \mathbf{2}} \frac{2}{4}$$

$$\frac{1}{2} = \frac{2}{4}$$

METHOD 2: *Making equivalent fractions by dividing:*

> ***Divide** the numerator and denominator of the given fraction by the same number.*

(You can only use this method when both the numerator and denominator can be divided by the same number.)

$$\frac{9}{12} \xrightarrow{\div \mathbf{3}} \frac{3}{4}$$

$$\frac{9}{12} = \frac{3}{4}$$

EXAMPLES OF HOW TO FIND EQUIVALENT FRACTIONS

1. Use Method 1. Multiply the numerator and denominator of the given fraction by the same number.

   For example, for the given fraction $\frac{2}{3}$, multiply the numerator and denominator by each of these numbers: 2, 3, 4, 5, and 6:

   $$\frac{2}{3} \xrightarrow{\times \mathbf{2}} \frac{4}{6}$$

   $$\frac{2}{3} \xrightarrow{\times \mathbf{3}} \frac{6}{9} \qquad\qquad \frac{2}{3} \xrightarrow{\times \mathbf{5}} \frac{10}{15}$$

   $$\frac{2}{3} \xrightarrow{\times \mathbf{4}} \frac{8}{12} \qquad\qquad \frac{2}{3} \xrightarrow{\times \mathbf{6}} \frac{12}{18}$$

   The fractions $\frac{4}{6}$, $\frac{6}{9}$, $\frac{8}{12}$, $\frac{10}{15}$, $\frac{12}{18}$ are equivalent to $\frac{2}{3}$.

33

2. SIMPLIFYING FRACTIONS

There is no end to the numbers you can use to multiply. So, there is an endless number of fractions equivalent to a given fraction.

2. Use Method 2. For example, find equivalent fractions for $\frac{40}{50}$.

Use the Divisibility Rules of *Lesson 2.2*.

Since 40 and 50 both end in 0, they can be divided by 2, 5, and 10. (See *Lesson 2.2* of this chapter.)

Here are three fractions equivalent to $\frac{40}{50}$:

$$\frac{40}{50} = \frac{20}{25} \quad \text{(Divide numerator and denominator of } \frac{40}{50} \text{ by 2)}$$

$$\frac{40}{50} = \frac{8}{10} \quad \text{(Divide numerator and denominator of } \frac{40}{50} \text{ by 5)}$$

$$\frac{40}{50} = \frac{4}{5} \quad \text{(Divide numerator and denominator by 10)}$$

Exercises with Hints

Are these fractions equivalent? Check (✓) the space to answer **yes** or **no**.

1. $\frac{1}{15}$ and $\frac{2}{30}$ ___ yes ___ no

(*Hint: Change $\frac{1}{15}$ to an equivalent fraction by **multiplying** both the numerator and denominator by 2. Notice that you can now compare this new fraction with $\frac{2}{30}$. Are they the same?*)

2. $\frac{9}{27}$ and $\frac{1}{3}$ ___ yes ___ no

(*Hint: Change $\frac{9}{27}$ to an equivalent fraction by **dividing** both the numerator and denominator by 9. Notice that you can now compare this new fraction with $\frac{1}{3}$. Are they the same?*)

3. $\frac{4}{5}$ and $\frac{28}{35}$ ___ yes ___ no

(*Hint: Change $\frac{4}{5}$ to an equivalent fraction by **multiplying** both the numerator and denominator by 7. Is this new fraction the same as $\frac{28}{35}$?*)

4. $\frac{24}{36}$ and $\frac{6}{12}$ ___ yes ___ no

(*Hint: Divide both numerator and denominator of $\frac{24}{36}$ by 3. Compare with $\frac{6}{12}$.*)

Use divisibility rules to change these fractions to equivalent fractions with denominators of 5.

5. $\frac{15}{25}$ _____

(*Hint: Divide both the numerator and the denominator by 5.*)

2.3 EQUIVALENT FRACTIONS—PART 1

6. $\frac{36}{45}$ (Hint: Divide by 9) _____

7. $\frac{63}{35}$ (Hint: Divide by 7) _____

Change these fractions to equivalent fractions with denominators of 16.

8. $\frac{1}{4}$ _____

(Hint: Multiply both the numerator and the denominator by 4)

9. $\frac{1}{2}$ (Hint: Multiply by 8) _____

10. $\frac{5}{8}$ (Hint: Multiply by 2) _____

11. Use divisibilty rules to find three fractions equivalent to $\frac{30}{50}$.

(Hint: Divide both the numerator and denominator by 2, 5, and 10.)

a. _____

b. _____

c. _____

Solve.

12. Ernie measured the distance between two nails on the wall twice. The first time he measured the distance he said it was $\frac{3}{4}$ foot. The second time he measured it he said it was $\frac{9}{12}$ foot. Are $\frac{3}{4}$ and $\frac{9}{12}$ equivalent fractions?

(Hint: Change $\frac{3}{4}$ to an equivalent fraction with the denominator of 12. Do this by multiplying both numerator and denominator of $\frac{3}{4}$ by 3. Then compare with $\frac{9}{12}$.)

___ yes ___ no

Exercises on Your Own

Are these pairs of fractions equivalent? Use the suggested method to find out. Check **yes** or **no**.

1. $\frac{1}{7}$ and $\frac{2}{14}$ ___ yes ___ no

(Multiply the numerator and denominator of $\frac{1}{7}$ by 2.)

2. $\frac{1}{4}$ and $\frac{5}{16}$ ___ yes ___ no

(Multiply the numerator and denominator of $\frac{1}{4}$ by 4.)

3. $\frac{5}{25}$ and $\frac{1}{5}$ ___ yes ___ no

(Divide the numerator and denominator of $\frac{5}{25}$ by 5)

4. $\frac{3}{20}$ and $\frac{9}{50}$ ___ yes ___ no

(Multiply the numerator and denominator of $\frac{3}{20}$ by 3. Notice that this time you will be comparing fractions with the same numerators, not the same denominators.)

35

2. SIMPLIFYING FRACTIONS

5. $\frac{10}{60}$ and $\frac{1}{6}$ ___ yes ___ no

(Divide the numerator and denominator of $\frac{10}{60}$ by 10.)

6. $\frac{3}{6}$ and $\frac{8}{18}$ ___ yes ___ no

(Multiply the numerator and denominator of $\frac{3}{6}$ by 3.)

7. Change $\frac{15}{20}$ to an equivalent fraction with a denominator of 4 by dividing both numerator and denominator by 5. $\frac{15}{20} =$ _____

8. Change $\frac{18}{24}$ to an equivalent fraction with a denominator of 4 by dividing both numerator and denominator by 6. $\frac{18}{24} =$ _____

9. Change $\frac{3}{4}$ to an equivalent fraction with a denominator of 12 by multiplying both numerator and denominator by 3. $\frac{3}{4} =$ _____

10. Change $\frac{7}{8}$ to an equivalent fraction with a denominator of 24 by multiplying both numerator and denominator by 3. $\frac{7}{8} =$ _____

11. Change $\frac{3}{5}$ to an equivalent fraction with a denominator of 25 by multiplying both numerator and denominator by 5. $\frac{3}{5} =$ _____

12. Change $\frac{16}{20}$ to an equivalent fraction with a denominator of 5 by dividing both numerator and denominator by 4. $\frac{16}{20} =$ _____

Use divisibility rules to change these fractions to equivalent fractions with denominators of 6.

13. $\frac{15}{18}$ *(Divide by 3)* _____

14. $\frac{25}{30}$ *(Divide by 5)* _____

15. $\frac{32}{48}$ *(Divide by 8)* _____

Solve.

16. Molly measured a ribbon for a package. She says it is $\frac{8}{10}$ meter. Jane says the ribbon is $\frac{4}{5}$ meter. Are these two lengths the same? *(Divide the numerator and denominator of $\frac{8}{10}$ by 2.)*

___ yes ___ no

17. Carlos and Maria both have to read 60 pages of history. Carlos did $\frac{2}{3}$ of the assignment and Maria did $\frac{5}{6}$ of the assignment. Did they do the same amount? *(Multiply the numerator and denominator of $\frac{2}{3}$ by 2.)*

___ yes ___ no

2.4 Equivalent Fractions—Part 2

Here is another lesson on how to find equivalent fractions. In this lesson, you will learn how to change a given fraction into an equivalent fraction.

- -

Valerie works for a drug company, where she has to make careful measurements of chemicals. She often has to change a fraction with one denominator to an equivalent fraction with another denominator. For example, she might have to change $\frac{3}{5}$ to tenths:

$$\frac{3}{5} = \frac{?}{10}$$

How does she do this?

Here are two rules that will help you do this. NOTICE THAT THESE RULES ARE THE SAME EXCEPT FOR STEP 2.

RULE 1: Finding the missing numerator of an equivalent fraction when the given denominator is the **smaller** denominator:

$$\frac{3}{5} = \frac{?}{10}$$

(The given fraction is $\frac{3}{5}$. The given denominator 5 is less than the denominator 10.)

1. **Divide the larger denominator by the smaller denominator:**

$$10 \div 5 = 2$$

2. **Multiply the given numerator by the result of Step 1. The answer is the missing numerator:**

$$3 \times 2 = 6$$

So $\frac{3}{5} = \frac{6}{10}$

RULE 2: Finding the missing numerator of an equivalent fraction when the given denominator is the **larger** denominator:

$$\frac{21}{28} = \frac{?}{4}$$

(Denominator 28 is larger than denominator 4)

1. **Divide the larger denominator by the smaller denominator:**

$$28 \div 4 = 7$$

2. SIMPLIFYING FRACTIONS

2. **Divide** the given numerator by the result of Step 1. The answer is the missing numerator:

$$21 \div 7 = 3$$

So $\dfrac{21}{28} = \dfrac{3}{4}$

EXAMPLES OF HOW TO FIND MISSING NUMERATORS

1. $\dfrac{2}{5} = \dfrac{?}{25}$

Given denominator 5 < 25, so Rule 1 applies.
Divide the larger denominator (25) by the smaller denominator (5):

$$25 \div 5 = 5.$$

Then multiply: $5 \times 2 = 10$.
The missing numerator is 10.

$$\dfrac{2}{5} = \dfrac{10}{25}$$

2. $\dfrac{30}{42} = \dfrac{?}{7}$

Given denominator 42 > 7, so Rule 2 applies.
Divide the larger denominator (42) by the smaller denominator (6):

$$42 \div 7 = 6.$$

Then divide: $30 \div 6 = 5$.
The missing numerator is 5.

$$\dfrac{30}{42} = \dfrac{5}{7}$$

Exercises with Hints

Which rule do you use to find the missing numerator? Check (✔) **Rule 1** or **2**. *(Hint: Which fraction has the larger denominator—the given fraction or the one whose numerator you have to find?)*

1. $\dfrac{5}{8} = \dfrac{?}{40}$ Rule 1 ___ Rule 2 ___

2. $\dfrac{5}{20} = \dfrac{?}{4}$ Rule 1 ___ Rule 2 ___

3. $\dfrac{9}{10} = \dfrac{?}{90}$ Rule 1 ___ Rule 2 ___

What is the first step in finding the missing numerator? *(Hint: Which numbers do you divide?)*

4. $\dfrac{2}{5} = \dfrac{?}{40}$ _____

5. $\dfrac{1}{7} = \dfrac{?}{49}$ _____

6. $\dfrac{56}{72} = \dfrac{?}{9}$ _____

38

2.4 EQUIVALENT FRACTIONS—PART 2

Write the numerators that will make the fractions equivalent.

7. $\frac{3}{5} = \frac{?}{10}$ _____ (Hint: Multiply by 2)

8. $\frac{24}{28} = \frac{?}{7}$ _____ (Hint: Divide by 4)

9. $\frac{4}{11} = \frac{?}{33}$ _____ (Hint: 33 ÷ 11 = ?)

10. $\frac{50}{60} = \frac{?}{6}$ _____ (Hint: 60 ÷ 6 = ?)

Solve.

11. Doug ate $\frac{5}{8}$ of a pizza. Did he eat more than $\frac{1}{2}$ of the pizza?

(Hint: $\frac{1}{2} = \frac{?}{8}$, then compare to $\frac{5}{8}$.)

_____

Exercises on Your Own

Which rule do you use to find the missing numerators? Check (✔) **Rule 1** or **2**.

1. $\frac{3}{10} = \frac{?}{20}$ Rule 1 ____ Rule 2 ____

2. $\frac{4}{14} = \frac{?}{7}$ Rule 1 ____ Rule 2 ____

3. $\frac{2}{3} = \frac{?}{9}$ Rule 1 ____ Rule 2 ____

Write the numerators that will make the fractions equivalent.

4. $\frac{1}{3} = \frac{?}{6}$ _____

5. $\frac{1}{6} = \frac{?}{12}$ _____

6. $\frac{3}{12} = \frac{?}{4}$ _____

7. $\frac{6}{7} = \frac{?}{21}$ _____

8. $\frac{3}{8} = \frac{?}{40}$ _____

9. $\frac{50}{70} = \frac{?}{7}$ _____

Solve.

10. Pedro wanted to find the number of minutes in $\frac{5}{6}$ of an hour, so he changed the fraction to an equivalent fraction with a denominator of 60. The numerator is the number of minutes. How many minutes in $\frac{5}{6}$ hour?

_____

11. Michael measured the width of a carpet and said that it was $\frac{30}{36}$ of a yard. To read this fraction more easily, change the fraction to a fraction with a denominator of 6.

_____

12. Norma added 12 ounces of flour to her special recipe. She calculated that this was $\frac{12}{16}$ of a pound. Write this fraction with a denominator of 4.

_____

2.5 Simplifying Fractions

When you do math with fractions, you often have to change a fraction with a large denominator into an equivalent fraction with a small denominator. For example, you might have to change $\frac{50}{100}$ into its equivalent, $\frac{1}{2}$.

This is called **reducing** or **simplifying** a fraction. The lesson will show you how to do it.

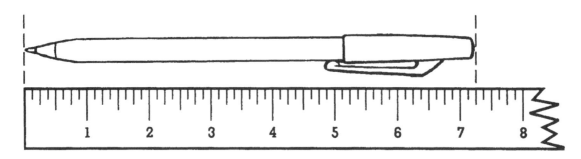

Lonnie measured his pen with a ruler. He says that it is $7\frac{2}{8}$ inches long. But he writes a fraction simpler than $7\frac{2}{8}$. What fraction does he write?

A fraction simpler than $\frac{2}{8}$ is a fraction equivalent to $\frac{2}{8}$ with a smaller numerator and denominator.

To find a simpler fraction, divide both numerator and denominator by 2:

$$\frac{2 \longrightarrow \div 2 \longrightarrow 1}{8 \longrightarrow \div 2 \longrightarrow 4}$$

- $\frac{1}{4}$ is simpler than $\frac{2}{8}$.

- Lonnie writes $7\frac{1}{4}$ instead of $7\frac{2}{8}$.

We say that $\frac{2}{8}$ has been simplified or reduced to $\frac{1}{4}$.

EXAMPLES

1. What is the *simplest* fraction equivalent to $\frac{25}{30}$?

    Divide the numerator and denominator by the greatest number that divides both 25 and 30.

    1 divides every number.

    Which numbers other than 1 divide both 25 and 30?
    (Use the Divisibility Rules of *Lesson 2.2*.)

2.5 SIMPLIFYING FRACTIONS

If a number ends in 0 or 5, then it can be divided by 5.
So, both 25 and 30 can be divided by 5:

$$\frac{25 \longrightarrow \div \mathbf{5} \longrightarrow 5}{30 \longrightarrow \div \mathbf{5} \longrightarrow 6}$$

$\frac{5}{6}$ cannot be reduced. It is the simplest fraction for $\frac{25}{30}$.

2. What is the *simplest* fraction equivalent to $\frac{12}{18}$?

Divide by the greatest number that divides both 12 and 18.

What numbers other than 1 divide both 12 and 18?
(Use the Divisibility Rules of *Lesson 2.2.*)

- The numbers that divide 12 are *1, 2, 3, 4, 6,* and *12.*
- The numbers that divide 18 are *1, 2, 3, 6, 9,* and *18.*
- The greatest number that divides both 12 and 18 is *6.*

$$\frac{12 \longrightarrow \div \mathbf{6} \longrightarrow 2}{18 \longrightarrow \div \mathbf{6} \longrightarrow 3}$$

$\frac{2}{3}$ is the simplest fraction for $\frac{12}{18}$.

A simplest fraction cannot be reduced.

RULE *for finding the simplest fraction:*

> **Divide by the greatest number that divides both the numerator
> and the denominator.**

Exercises with Hints

1. Circle all the numbers that divide both 6 and 18. (Hint: Use the divisibility rules. Why doesn't 12 work?)

1 2 3 4 6 9 12

2. Which is the greatest number that divides both 6 and 18? *(Hint: Look at the list of the answers to Exercise 1, then circle the greatest.)*

1 2 3 4 6 9 12

3. Reduce $\frac{6}{18}$ to the simplest fraction. *(Hint: Divide both 6 and 18 by the answer to Exercise 2.)*

_____

4. What number do you divide into 24 and 30 to reduce $\frac{24}{30}$ to the simplest fraction? *(Hint: Find the greatest number that divides both 24 and 30.)*

a. 2   c. 6

b. 4   d. 12

2. SIMPLIFYING FRACTIONS

5. What is the simplest fraction for $\frac{24}{30}$?
(Hint: Divide by the answer to Exercise 4.)

_____

6. What is the simplest fraction for $\frac{30}{40}$?
(Hint: What is the greatest number that divides 30 and 40?)

_____

Solve.

7. Jose wants to write the simplest fraction for $\frac{8}{24}$. What fraction should he write? *(Hint: What number should he divide by?)*

_____

8. Calvin read 4 pages of a 100-page book. What fraction of the book did he read? Reduce your answer to the simplest fraction. *(Hint: Write the fraction first, then use divisibility rules.)*

_____

Exercises on Your Own

1. Which numbers besides 1 divide both 10 and 20?

_____

2. Which is the greatest number that divides both 10 and 20?

_____

3. What is the simplest fraction for $\frac{10}{20}$?

_____

4. Which numbers besides 1 divide both 9 and 36?

_____

5. Which is the greatest number that divides both 9 and 36?

_____

6. What is the simplest fraction for $\frac{9}{36}$?

_____

7. What is the simplest fraction for $\frac{22}{33}$?

_____

8. What is the simplest fraction for $\frac{16}{20}$?

_____

Solve.

9. Carla said that $\frac{18}{30}$ of the month had gone by. Reduce $\frac{18}{30}$ to the simplest fraction.

_____

10. Frank played his CD player for fifteen minutes—$\frac{15}{60}$ of an hour. What is the simplest fraction for $\frac{15}{60}$?

_____

11. Molly has $72 of the $108 she need to pay for a set of curtains. What fraction of the total does she have? Reduce the fraction to the simplest fraction.

_____

2.6 Greatest Common Factor (GCF)

A number that can be divided evenly into another number is called a *factor* of the second number. For example, 2 is a factor of 10, since 2 divides into 10 with no remainder.

When you reduce fractions, you are dividing by a factor of both the numerator and the denominator—called a *common factor.* This lesson will tell you more about common factors. It will also tell you about the *greatest common factor* of two numbers.

Art asks Doug if he knows a number that is a factor of both 12 and 16.

Doug says, "What is a factor?"

Art explains that the *factors* of a given number are the numbers that can be divided evenly into it. Or, to put it another way, they are numbers that are multiplied to produce the given number.

For example, two of the factors of 12 are 3 and 4 because—

    —Both 3 and 4 divide evenly into 12.

    —And because $3 \times 4 = 12$.

Doug starts to think. Then he makes these two lists of all the numbers you can multiply together to get 12 and 16. He makes one list for 12 and another for 16.

Multiplication Sentences for 12	Multiplication Sentences for 16
$1 \times 12 = 12$	$1 \times 16 = 16$
$2 \times 6 = 12$	$2 \times 8 = 16$
$3 \times 4 = 12$	$4 \times 4 = 16$

From these lists, Art makes lists of all the factors of the two numbers:

Factors of 12: *1, 2, 3, 4, 6, 12*

Factors of 16: *1, 2, 4, 8, 16*

Doug notices that the the numbers 1, 2, and 4 are on both lists of factors.

These are called the *common factors* of the numbers 12 and 16.

The number 4 is the largest factor of both 12 and 16. It is called the *greatest common factor,* or *GCF,* of both numbers. The GCF of 12 and 16 is 4.

2. SIMPLIFYING FRACTIONS

RULE: *How to find the GCF of two numbers:*

> 1. **List all the factors of the first number.**
>
> 2. **List all the factors of the second number.**
>
> 3. **Find the common factors (the factors of both numbers).**
>
> 4. **The largest number on <u>both</u> lists is the greatest common factor—the GCF.**

EXAMPLE

Find the GCF of 10 and 30.

1. List the factors of 10: *1, 2, 5, 10*
2. List the factors of 30: *1, 2, 3, 5, 6, 10, 30*
3. The common factors of 10 and 30 are *1, 2, 5,* and *10.*
4. The greatest common factor (GCF) of 10 and 30 is 10. It's the largest number on both lists.

Exercises with Hints

(Hint: For Exercises 1-5, find out which numbers divide evenly into the given number. They are the factors.)

1. Which of these numbers are factors of 6? Circle them. (Hint: The given number is 6. What 4 numbers divide into it evenly?)

    1 2 3 4 5 6

2. Which of these numbers are factors of 15? Circle them. (Hint: There are 4 factors.)

    1 2 3 4 5 9 10 15

3. Which of these numbers are factors of 22? (Hint: There are 4 factors.)

    1 2 3 4 6 11 12 22

4. List all the factors of 8.
    (Hint: There are 4 of them.)

    _____

5. List all the factors of 12.
    (Hint: There are 6 of them.)

    _____

6. What are the common factors of 8 and 12? (Hint: Find the factors of Exercises 4 and 5 that are the same.)

    _____

7. What is the GCF of 8 and 12? (Hint: Find the greatest factor of Exercise 6.)

    _____

44

2.6 GREATEST COMMON FACTOR (GCF)

8. List the factors of 16.
(*Hint: There are 5.*)

_____

9. List the factors of 20.
(*Hint: There are 6 of them.*)

_____

10. What are the common factors of 16
and 20? (*Hint: Find the factors that
appear in both Exercises 8 and 9.*)

_____

11. What is the GCF of 16 and 20?
(*Hint: Find the greatest factor of
Exercise 10.*)

_____

Exercises on Your Own

List all the factors of each number.

1. 14 _____

2. 18 _____

3. 21 _____

4. 32 _____

5. 75 _____

6. 35 _____

7. 40 _____

8. 42 _____

9. 49 _____

10. 63 _____

List the common factors of each pair of
numbers. Use your answers to Exercises
1-10 to help you.

11. 14 and 18 _____

12. 21 and 32 _____

13. 35 and 75 _____

14. 40 and 42 _____

15. 49 and 63 _____

Find the GCF of each pair of numbers.
Use your answers to Exercises 10-15
to help you.

16. 14 and 18 _____

17. 21 and 32 _____

18. 35 and 75 _____

19. 40 and 42 _____

20. 49 and 63 _____

2.7 Two Ways of Simplifying Fractions

What is the best way to simplify a fraction? This lesson will show you two ways. Use the one that works best for you.

Harry counted 42 boys and girls on a bus. He figured out that $\frac{30}{42}$ of the students were boys.

Write this fraction in simplest form.

To reduce $\frac{30}{42}$ to the simplest form, divide both numerator and denominator by the same number.

There are two ways to reduce a fraction to simplest form.

METHOD 1. Divide by the greatest common factor (GCF)

In this method you find the GCF. Then you reduce $\frac{30}{42}$ by dividing both the numerator and denominator by the GCF.

Find the GCF of 30 and 42.
- List the factors of 30: *1, 2, 3, 5, 6, 10, 15, 30*
- List the factors of 42: *1, 2, 6, 7, 21, 42*
- Now list the common factors of 30 and 42: *1, 2, 6.*

The greatest number in this list is 6.

So the GCF of 30 and 42 is 6.

Divide 30 and 42 by 6:

$$\frac{30}{42} \longrightarrow \frac{30 \div 6}{42 \div 6} \longrightarrow \frac{5}{7}$$

$\frac{5}{7}$ is the simplest fraction that is equivalent to $\frac{30}{42}$ because the only number that divides 5 and 7 is 1.

When you simplify a fraction with the GCF, you reduce the fraction to the simplest fraction in one step. But it can take a long time to list all the factors of the original fraction. For this reason, you should also know how to use Method 2, which follows.

METHOD 2. *Divide both numerator and denominator by common factors as often as you can.*

In this method, you divide both the numerator and denominator of $\frac{30}{42}$ by *any* common factor.

You can start with a small factor, but be prepared to do this procedure more than once before you reduce the fraction to the simplest fraction. The divisibility rules of *Lesson 2.2* can be very helpful.

For example, here's how to simplify $\frac{30}{42}$, using Method 2.

- Since 30 and 42 are even numbers (numbers that end in 0, 2, 4, 6, or 8), they are divisible by 2:

$$\frac{30}{42} = \frac{30 \div \mathbf{2}}{42 \div \mathbf{2}} = \frac{15}{21}$$

- But $\frac{15}{21}$ is *not* the simplest fraction! You have to divide again. Use the divisibility rules again to find another common factor. You find that 3 divides both 15 and 21. (The sum of the digits of 15 and 21 is divisible by 3).

$$\frac{15}{21} = \frac{15 \div \mathbf{3}}{21 \div \mathbf{3}} = \frac{5}{7}$$

There is no common factor of 3 and 7. So $\frac{5}{7}$ cannot be simplified any more.

EXAMPLE USING *METHOD 1*

Find the simplest fraction that is equivalent to $\frac{45}{60}$.

Find the GCF of 45 and 60:

- Factors of 45: *1, 3, 5, 9, 15, 45*
- Factors of 60: *1, 2, 3, 4, 5, 6, 10, 12, 15, 20, 30, 60*

The GCF of 45 and 60 is 15.

Divide 45 and 60 by 15:

$$\frac{45}{60} = \frac{45 \div \mathbf{15}}{60 \div \mathbf{15}} = \frac{3}{4}$$

$\frac{3}{4}$ is the simplest fraction that is equivalent to $\frac{45}{60}$.

2. SIMPLIFYING FRACTIONS

EXAMPLE USING *METHOD 2*

Find the simplest fraction equivalent to $\frac{48}{108}$.

- Since both numerator and denominator are even numbers, divide them by 2:

$$\frac{48}{108} = \frac{48 \div \mathbf{2}}{108 \div \mathbf{2}} = \frac{24}{54}$$

- Since 24 and 54 are both divisible by 3 (the sum of the digits of 24 and 54 is divisible by 3), then:

$$\frac{24}{54} = \frac{24 \div \mathbf{3}}{54 \div \mathbf{3}} = \frac{8}{18}$$

- Both 8 and 18 are even numbers and divisible by 2:

$$\frac{8}{18} = \frac{8 \div \mathbf{2}}{18 \div \mathbf{2}} = \frac{4}{9}$$

$\frac{4}{9}$ cannot be reduced any more, so it is the simplest fraction equivalent to $\frac{48}{108}$.

It took three steps to reduce the fraction $\frac{48}{108}$ to simplest terms, but it doesn't take long.

Exercises with Hints _____

List the factors of each number.
(Hint: *Look back at the Divisibility Rules* in Lesson 2.2 *if you need to.*)

1. 14 _____

2. 22 _____

3. 16 _____

4. 40 _____

5. 25 _____

6. 125 _____

Find the GCF of each pair of numbers.
(Hint: *Use the results of Exercises 1-6.*)

7. 14, 22 _____

8. 16, 40 _____

9. 25, 125 _____

10. 25, 40 _____

Use Method 1 to reduce each fraction to the simplest fraction.
(Hint: *Use the results of Exercises 1-10.*)

11. $\frac{14}{22}$ _____

12. $\frac{16}{40}$ _____

13. $\frac{25}{125}$ _____

14. $\frac{25}{40}$ _____

2.7 TWO WAYS OF SIMPLIFYING FRACTIONS

Use Method 2 to reduce each fraction to simplest fractions *(Hint: Use the divisibility rules of Lesson 2.2. You'll need to divide more than once.)*

15. $\frac{16}{48}$ _____

16. $\frac{12}{80}$ _____

17. $\frac{35}{140}$ _____

18. $\frac{75}{120}$ _____

Solve.

19. Harry's records showed that 32 out of 100 people he surveyed were smokers. What fraction of those surveyed are smokers? Reduce this fraction to its simplest fraction. *(Hint: Use either method to reduce the fraction.)*

_____

Exercises on Your Own

Find the GCF of each pair of numbers.

1. 30, 45 _____

2. 24, 60 _____

3. 36, 90 _____

4. 35, 84 _____

Use the GCF of Exercises 1-4 to reduce these fractions to simplest form.

5. $\frac{30}{45}$ _____

6. $\frac{24}{60}$ _____

7. $\frac{36}{90}$ _____

8. $\frac{35}{84}$ _____

Use either method to reduce these fractions to simplest form.

9. $\frac{18}{54}$ _____

10. $\frac{26}{65}$ _____

11. $\frac{48}{60}$ _____

12. $\frac{63}{108}$ _____

Solve.

13. Bill said that 27 people of the 90 people on his floor will join the bowling league. What fraction will join the bowling league? Reduce this fraction to the simplest fraction.

_____

14. Anita was late 8 of 64 days during the last quarter. The fraction of days she came late is $\frac{8}{64}$. Reduce this fraction to simplest form.

_____

2.8 Review

Write the missing numerators. Shade the rectangles to help you if you wish.

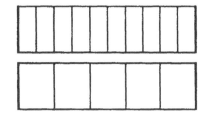

1. $\frac{4}{10} = \frac{}{5}$

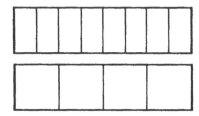

2. $\frac{2}{8} = \frac{}{4}$

Are these numbers divisible by **5**?

3. 72 ___ yes ___ no
4. 85 ___ yes ___ no
5. 215 ___ yes ___ no

Are these numbers divisible by **3**?

6. 36 ___ yes ___ no
7. 832 ___ yes ___ no
8. 177 ___ yes ___ no

Are these numbers divisible by **2**?

9. 406 ___ yes ___ no
10. 327 ___ yes ___ no
11. 1503 ___ yes ___ no

Are these numbers divisible by **10**?

12. 30 ___ yes ___ no
13. 155 ___ yes ___ no
14. 640 ___ yes ___ no

Are these numbers divisible by **9**?

15. 45 ___ yes ___ no
16. 207 ___ yes ___ no
17. 2375 ___ yes ___ no

For Exercises 18 and 19, find out if the fractions are equivalent. Follow the suggestions to find out.

18. $\frac{3}{8}$ and $\frac{8}{24}$ ___ yes ___ no

    (Hint: Multiply the numerator and denominator of $\frac{3}{8}$ by 3.)

19. $\frac{6}{36}$ and $\frac{1}{6}$ ___ yes ___ no

    (Hint: Divide the numerator and denominator of $\frac{6}{36}$ by 6.)

20. Change $\frac{12}{24}$ to an equivalent fraction with a denominator of 4 by dividing the numerator and denominator by 6.

    $\frac{12}{24} = $ _____

21. Change $\frac{1}{6}$ to a fraction with a denominator of 24 by multiplying the numerator and denominator by 4.

    $\frac{1}{6} = $ _____

2.8 REVIEW

Use divisibility rules to change these fractions to equivalent fractions with denominators of 5.

22. $\frac{20}{25}$ *(Divide by 5)* _____

23. $\frac{9}{15}$ *(Divide by 3)* _____

Find the numerators that will make the fractions equivalent.

24. $\frac{1}{7} = \frac{?}{14}$ _____

25. $\frac{3}{8} = \frac{?}{24}$ _____

26. $\frac{60}{70} = \frac{?}{7}$ _____

27. $\frac{2}{5} = \frac{?}{40}$ _____

28. $\frac{3}{27} = \frac{?}{9}$ _____

29. Which numbers besides 1 divide both 12 and 18? _____

30. Which is the greatest number that divides both 12 and 18?

_____

31. What is the simplest fraction for $\frac{12}{18}$? _____

32. What is the simplest fraction for $\frac{10}{25}$? _____

33. What is the simplest fraction for $\frac{20}{32}$? _____

List the factors of each number.

34. 24 _____

35. 27 _____

36. 40 _____

List the common factors of each pair of numbers.

37. 21 and 28 _____

38. 15 and 30 _____

39. 56 and 72 _____

Find the GCF of each pair of numbers.

40. 15, 45 _____

41. 10, 12 _____

42. 35, 55 _____

43. 42, 70 _____

Use the GCF of Exercises 41-44 to reduce these fractions to simplest form.

44. $\frac{15}{45}$ _____

45. $\frac{10}{12}$ _____

46. $\frac{35}{55}$ _____

47. $\frac{42}{70}$ _____

Simplify these fractions completely.

48. $\frac{45}{54}$ _____

49. $\frac{10}{45}$ _____

50. $\frac{18}{32}$ _____

51. $\frac{20}{36}$ _____

Solve.

52. Rosa has 72 bottles that she wants to divide into equal groups.

    a. Can she divide the bottles into 2 equal groups?

    ____ yes ____ no

    b. Into 3 equal groups?

    ____ yes ____ no

    c. Into 5 equal groups?

    ____ yes ____ no

    d. Into 9 equal groups?

    ____ yes ____ no

    e. Into 10 equal groups?

    ____ yes ____ no

53. Erica ran $\frac{6}{8}$ of a mile. Write this fraction with a denominator of 4.

_____

54. Dennis waited $\frac{1}{3}$ hour for a ticket to a basketball game. Change this fraction to an equivalent fraction with a denominator of 60.

_____

55. Mabel moved 12 of the 30 boxes in the warehouse.

    a. What fraction of the boxes did she move? _____

    b. Write this fraction in simplest form. _____

56. Anita did not show up to work on 5 of the 20 working days last month.

    a. Write a fraction that shows the part of the time she did not show up for work.

_____

    b. Write this fraction in simplest form. _____

3. **Mixed Numbers**

3.1 Fractions Less Than, Equal To, and Greater Than 1

The fractions you have been working with are all less than 1. For example, $\frac{1}{2}$, $\frac{2}{3}$, and $\frac{5}{9}$ are all less than 1.

In this lesson you will learn something about fractions that are equal to 1 or that are greater than 1.

Mark draws comic strips for a newspaper. He finished one strip this morning and is working on a second strip. Each comic strip is divided into 4 equal parts. That is, each strip is divided into fourths.

How many fourths are in 1 strip?

- Count the number of fourths. There are 4 fourths in 1 strip.

You write $\frac{4}{4}$ for 4 fourths. $\frac{4}{4} = 1$

RULE:

> *If the numerator and the denominator are equal, the fraction equals 1.*

How many fourths are filled altogether in the **two** strips?

- Count the total number of fourths with pictures in them.

- There are 6 fourths that are filled.

You write $\frac{6}{4}$ for 6 fourths.

$$\frac{6}{4} > 1$$

RULE:

> **If the numerator is greater than the denominator, the fraction is greater than 1.**

SPECIAL NOTE: Fractions greater than 1 are sometimes called *improper fractions*. This book doesn't use this name, but you should know it in case you see it again.

- -

How many fourths are **not** filled?

- Count them.

- There are 2 fourths that are not filled.

So $\frac{2}{4} < 1$

RULE:

> **If the numerator is less than the denominator, the fraction is less than 1.**

EXAMPLES

Fractions less than 1: $\frac{1}{2}, \frac{5}{6}, \frac{2}{10}, \frac{4}{9}, \frac{45}{46}$

(Numerator *less than* denominator)

Fractions equal to 1: $\frac{4}{4}, \frac{7}{7}, \frac{98}{98}$

(Numerator *equal to* denominator)

Fractions greater than 1: $\frac{5}{4}, \frac{18}{3}, \frac{25}{1}, \frac{76}{70}$

(Numerator *greater than* denominator)

3.1 FRACTIONS LESS THAN, EQUAL TO, AND GREATER THAN 1

Exercises with Hints

For which fractions is the numerator greater than the denominator?
Put a check mark (✔) before them.
(Hint: The numerator is the number on top.)

1. ☐ $\frac{6}{6}$

2. ☐ $\frac{9}{8}$

3. ☐ $\frac{12}{3}$

4. ☐ $\frac{8}{10}$

Which fractions are greater than 1?
Put a check mark before them.
(Hint: The fraction is greater than 1 if the numerator is greater than the denominator.)

5. ☐ $\frac{7}{2}$

6. ☐ $\frac{6}{6}$

7. ☐ $\frac{5}{6}$

8. ☐ $\frac{9}{7}$

Which fractions are equal to 1?
Put a check mark before them.
(Hint: The fraction is equal to 1 if the numerator is equal to the denominator.)

9. ☐ $\frac{9}{9}$

10. ☐ $\frac{7}{8}$

11. ☐ $\frac{2}{2}$

12. ☐ $\frac{5}{4}$

Which fractions are less than 1?
Put a check mark before them.
(Hint: A fraction is less than 1 if the numerator is less than the denominator.)

13. ☐ $\frac{10}{7}$

14. ☐ $\frac{7}{10}$

15. ☐ $\frac{30}{30}$

16. ☐ $\frac{1}{11}$

Solve.

17. Ji-Reh noticed that the water level of the furnace gauge was about $\frac{5}{4}$ of the normal level. Was the water level above or below the normal level?

    (Hint: Is $\frac{5}{4} > 1$ or is $\frac{5}{4} < 1$?)

    _____

    _____

3. MIXED NUMBERS

Exercises on Your Own

Circle the fractions that are less than 1.

1. $\frac{9}{10}$

2. $\frac{4}{9}$

3. $\frac{7}{7}$

4. $\frac{9}{6}$

Circle the fractions that equal 1.

5. $\frac{6}{6}$

6. $\frac{7}{3}$

7. $\frac{3}{3}$

8. $\frac{9}{10}$

Circle the fractions that are greater than 1.

9. $\frac{3}{3}$

10. $\frac{3}{4}$

11. $\frac{4}{3}$

12. $\frac{25}{2}$

Compare these fractions by writing **<**, **=**, or **>** in each blank.

13. $\frac{4}{4}$ ___ $\frac{7}{6}$

14. $\frac{13}{5}$ ___ $\frac{7}{9}$

15. $\frac{7}{10}$ ___ $\frac{12}{12}$

Write these fractions in order from least to greatest.

16. $\frac{3}{2}$, $\frac{5}{5}$, $\frac{4}{5}$

_____

17. $\frac{7}{7}$, $\frac{7}{8}$, $\frac{8}{7}$

_____

18. $\frac{14}{3}$, $\frac{25}{25}$, $\frac{25}{26}$

_____

Solve.

19. Doug said that it took him $\frac{7}{8}$ of an hour to finish painting a set of shelves. Did it take more than an hour or less than an hour?

_____

20. Tani had an unusual week. She worked $\frac{5}{4}$ as may hours as she usually does. Did she work more or less than she usually does? Explain your answer.

_____

_____

_____

3.2 Identifying Mixed Numbers

In this lesson, you will learn about numbers like $3\frac{1}{4}$, which contain both a whole number part and a fraction part. They are called **mixed numbers**.

Donna filled two glasses with juice. Then she filled another glass half full with juice. Altogether, she has two and a half glasses of juice.

- You write two and a half as $2\frac{1}{2}$.
- You read $2\frac{1}{2}$ as "two and a half."

Donna has $2\frac{1}{2}$ glasses of juice.

$2\frac{1}{2}$ is called a **mixed number**.

A mixed number is made up of a whole number (like 2) and a fraction (like $\frac{1}{2}$).

> **EXAMPLES**
>
> These are examples of **whole numbers**:
>
> 0, 1, 2, 3, 4, and so on.
>
> These are examples of **fractions**:
>
> $\frac{2}{3}$, $\frac{7}{11}$, $\frac{14}{5}$, $\frac{7}{9}$, and $\frac{4}{4}$
>
> These are examples of **mixed numbers**:
>
> $4\frac{1}{5}$, $9\frac{2}{3}$, and $29\frac{7}{9}$
>
> These are *not* mixed numbers:
>
> $\frac{2}{4}$, $\frac{7}{2}$, 28, and 5.472

3. MIXED NUMBERS

Exercises with Hints

Put a check mark (✔) before the numbers that are **whole numbers.**
(Hint: The whole numbers are 0, 1, 2, 3, 4, and so on. A whole number does not have a fractional part.)

1. ☐ 19

2. ☐ $4\frac{1}{8}$

3. ☐ 451

4. ☐ $\frac{6}{13}$

5. ☐ 12,984

6. ☐ $\frac{7}{6}$

Put a check mark before the numbers that are **fractions.**
(Hint: A fraction is a number that has a numerator and a denominator. A fraction does not have a whole number part.)

7. ☐ $\frac{7}{3}$

8. ☐ $\frac{3}{7}$

9. ☐ $14\frac{1}{7}$

10. ☐ 194

11. ☐ $\frac{12}{12}$

12. ☐ $\frac{1}{8}$

Put a check mark before the numbers that are **mixed numbers.**
(Hint: A mixed number is a number made up of a whole number and a fraction.)

13. ☐ $45\frac{1}{9}$

14. ☐ 4,765

15. ☐ $8\frac{7}{8}$

16. ☐ $\frac{3}{5}$

17. ☐ $\frac{9}{3}$

18. ☐ $2\frac{4}{23}$

Write mixed numbers for each of these.
(Hint: Say the words to yourself, then write a whole number and a fraction.)

19. six and nine-tenths _____

20. one and five-sixths _____

Underline the mixed numbers in these sentences. Be sure to underline the *entire mixed number*, not just the fraction.

21. Gladys drove $\frac{3}{4}$ hour to the mall, shopped for $2\frac{1}{2}$ hours, spent $78.35, and ate 3 hamburgers. When she got home, she spoke on the phone for $\frac{1}{2}$ hour and napped for $1\frac{1}{2}$ hours.
(Hint: You should underline 2 numbers.)

58

Exercises on Your Own

Put a check mark (✔) before the numbers that are fractions.

1. ☐ $\frac{5}{11}$

2. ☐ $\frac{6}{6}$

3. ☐ $\frac{80}{5}$

4. ☐ $2\frac{9}{13}$

5. ☐ 0

6. ☐ $\frac{1}{2}$

Put a check mark before the numbers that are mixed numbers.

7. ☐ $7\frac{1}{8}$

8. ☐ $\frac{5}{4}$

9. ☐ $100\frac{1}{2}$

10. ☐ 400

11. ☐ $4\frac{7}{6}$

12. ☐ $\frac{2}{7}$

Check **true** or **false**.

13. A fraction does not have a whole number part.

____ true ____ false

14. A mixed number is made up of a whole number and a fraction.

____ true ____ false

15. A whole number has a fractional part.

____ true ____ false

Write mixed numbers for each of these:

16. seven and three-eighths _____

17. nineteen and four-fifths _____

Underline the mixed numbers in these sentences. Be sure to underline the *entire number,* not just the fraction.

18. Josh is $15\frac{3}{4}$ years old, and he can jump $1\frac{1}{10}$ meters off the ground, he can leap $5\frac{3}{10}$ meters, and he can throw a baseball 50 meters.

19. Harriet spoke for $3\frac{1}{2}$ minutes, used 17 slides and $4\frac{1}{2}$ pages of notes, and made 100 new friends.

Put these numbers in order from least to greatest.

20. $\frac{9}{9}$, $\frac{10}{11}$, $4\frac{1}{2}$

_____

21. $1\frac{1}{8}$, $\frac{7}{7}$, $\frac{1}{10}$

_____

22. $\frac{4}{5}$, $2\frac{2}{3}$, $\frac{5}{5}$

_____

3.3 Changing Improper Fractions Greater Than 1 to Mixed Numbers

Any fraction greater than 1—the fraction $\frac{12}{7}$, for example—can be changed to a mixed number. This lesson will show you how.

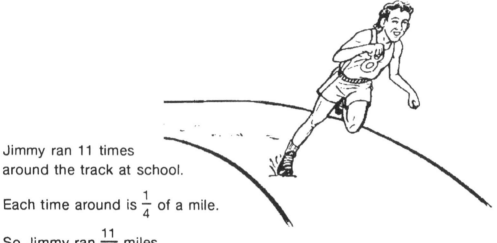

Jimmy ran 11 times around the track at school.

Each time around is $\frac{1}{4}$ of a mile.

So Jimmy ran $\frac{11}{4}$ miles.

$\frac{11}{4}$ is a fraction that is greater than 1.

Any fraction greater than 1 can also be changed to a mixed number. (This is sometimes called *renaming* it.)

How do you write (rename) $\frac{11}{4}$ miles as a mixed number?

- First divide the numerator (11) by the denominator (4).
- Then form a mixed number with the **quotient** and fractional **remainder:**

$$\begin{array}{r} 2 \\ 4\overline{)11} \\ -8 \\ \hline 3\,R \end{array}$$

⟶ **2** full miles (This is the **quotient**)

⟶ **remainder 3**. This means 3 times around the track, or $\frac{3}{4}$ of a mile—since each time around is $\frac{1}{4}$ mile.

The **fraction** $\frac{11}{4}$ miles is the same as the **mixed number** $2\frac{3}{4}$ miles.

3.3 CHANGING IMPROPER FRACTIONS GREATER THAN 1 TO MIXED NUMBERS

METHOD *for changing a fraction greater than 1 into a mixed number:*

1. **Divide the numerator by the denominator.**
   (You will get a whole number plus a remainder.)

2. **The remainder is the numerator of a new fraction that you write after the whole number.**

3. **The denominator of the new fraction is the same as the denominator of the original fraction.**
   (If there isn't any remainder, there isn't any new fraction. The answer is a <u>whole</u> number, not a <u>mixed</u> number. For example, $\frac{4}{2}$ is equal to 2.)

EXAMPLES

1. To change $\frac{16}{3}$ to a mixed number, divide 16 by 3:

$$
\begin{array}{r}
5 \quad \longleftarrow \text{ whole number part} \\
3\,)\,\overline{16} \\
-\,15 \\
\hline
1\ R \quad \longleftarrow \text{ use remainder to form fraction part}
\end{array}
$$

$$\text{Fraction part } = \frac{\text{remainder}}{\text{divisor}} = \frac{1}{3}$$

So $\frac{16}{3} = 5\frac{1}{3}$

2. To rename $\frac{37}{5}$ as a mixed number, divide 37 by 5:

$$
\begin{array}{r}
7 \\
5\,)\,\overline{37} \\
-\,35 \\
\hline
2\ R
\end{array}
$$

$$\frac{37}{5} = 7\frac{2}{5}$$

3. MIXED NUMBERS

Exercises with Hints

Choose the division example that will change the improper fraction to a mixed number, and circle the answer. *(Hint: Divide the numerator by the denominator.)*

1. $\frac{25}{2}$

   a. 12) 25

   b. 2) 25

   c. 25) 2

2. $\frac{95}{7}$

   a. 7) 95

   b. 95) 7

   c. 5) 95

3. $\frac{40}{6}$

   a. 40) 40

   b. 40) 6

   c. 6) 40

Divide to change these fractions greater than 1 to mixed numbers. What is the whole number part? Circle the answer. *(Hint: Just find the whole number part. Don't worry about the remainder in this question.)*

4. $\frac{27}{6}$

   a. 3

   b. 4

   c. 5

5. $\frac{41}{8}$

   a. 4

   b. 5

   c. 6

6. $\frac{38}{7}$

   a. 3

   b. 4

   c. 5

Change each improper fraction to a mixed number.
(Hint: Divide numerator by denominator.)

7. $\frac{14}{3}$ _____

8. $\frac{15}{4}$ _____

9. $\frac{22}{8}$ _____

10. $\frac{17}{5}$ _____

11. $\frac{38}{9}$ _____

Solve.

12. Felix spent his day off cooking and baking. He uses a $\frac{1}{3}$ cup measure to measure how much of each ingredient he should use. For one recipe, he filled the cup 7 times with water. How many cups of water did he use?
(Hint: Write a fraction, then rename it as a mixed number.)

_____

3.3 CHANGING IMPROPER FRACTIONS GREATER THAN 1 TO MIXED NUMBERS

Exercises on Your Own _____

Which of these fractions are equivalent to whole numbers, not mixed numbers? Put a check mark in front of them.

1. ☐ $\frac{30}{6}$

2. ☐ $\frac{22}{7}$

3. ☐ $\frac{19}{5}$

4. ☐ $\frac{18}{3}$

5. ☐ $\frac{16}{4}$

Change each fraction greater than 1 to a mixed number.

6. $\frac{9}{2}$ _____

7. $\frac{14}{3}$ _____

8. $\frac{25}{8}$ _____

9. $\frac{44}{10}$ _____

10. $\frac{65}{8}$ _____

Solve.

11. Greg said he used $\frac{11}{2}$ cups of flour to make cookies. Change this fraction to a mixed number.

_____

12. Toby works part time at the super market. She works $\frac{1}{3}$ of a day each time she works. How many days does she work after 10 days at the super market? (Put your answer in the form of a mixed number.)

_____

13. Josephine ordered several pizzas for a party. She divided each pizza into 8 equal pieces for the party. At the end of the party there were 13 pieces left. Write a mixed number for the amount of pizza left over.

_____

3.4 Rounding Mixed Numbers

Sometimes you may be asked to *"round a mixed number to the nearest whole number."* This lesson will show you how.

Fran wrote a paper on a word processor. It was $5\frac{1}{4}$ pages long. About how long was the paper to *the nearest whole number?*

Round $5\frac{1}{4}$ to *the nearest whole number.*

There are two ways to do this: The **Number Line Method** and the **Numerator-Denominator Method.**

THE NUMBER LINE METHOD

Here's how to use the Number Line Method to help round numbers to *the nearest whole number.*

Look at the number line:

$5\frac{1}{4}$ is nearer to 5 than to 6.

So $5\frac{1}{4}$ rounded to the *nearest* whole number is 5.

The paper is about 5 pages long.

RULE:

> - *If the fraction part of the mixed number is $\frac{1}{2}$ or greater than $\frac{1}{2}$, then round to the next higher whole number.*
> - *If the fraction part of the whole number is less than $\frac{1}{2}$, just drop the fraction.*

64

3.4 ROUNDING MIXED NUMBERS

> **EXAMPLE 1**
>
> Raheem measured the length of his computer table and said it was $2\frac{7}{8}$ feet long. Round this number *to the nearest foot*.
>
> Use the Number Line Method.
>
>
>
> $2\frac{7}{8}$ is nearer to 3 than to 2.
>
> $2\frac{7}{8}$ rounded to the nearest whole number is 3.

THE NUMERATOR-DENOMINATOR METHOD

Besides the number line, there is another way to find if a fraction is less than or greater than $\frac{1}{2}$.

Multiply the numerator of the fraction by 2 and compare this product to the denominator.

RULE:

> - *If the product is <u>greater</u> than the denominator, the fraction is greater than $\frac{1}{2}$.*
>
> - *If the product is <u>less</u> than the denominator, then the fraction is less than $\frac{1}{2}$.*

> **EXAMPLE 2**
>
> Georgette rehearsed $5\frac{3}{5}$ hours for the play. About how many hours did she rehearse?
>
> Round $5\frac{3}{5}$ to *the nearest whole number*.
>
> - $5\frac{3}{5}$ is between 5 and 6.
> - Applying the Numerator-Denominator method to $\frac{3}{5}$, multiply the numerator × 2: 3 × 2 = 6
> - Compare the product with the denominator: 6 > 5

65

So $\frac{3}{5} > \frac{1}{2}$

$5\frac{3}{5}$ is more than halfway from 5 to 6.

$5\frac{3}{5}$ rounded to the *nearest* whole number is 6.

Exercises with Hints

Use the Number Line Method to round these mixed numbers to the nearest whole number.
(Hint: Divide each unit of the number line into fourths. Then find the correct place on the line for each of the numbers below.)

1. $6\frac{1}{4}$ is about _____

2. $3\frac{3}{4}$ is about _____

3. $1\frac{3}{4}$ is about _____

Round each of these mixed numbers to the nearest whole number.
(Hint: Use the Numerator-Denominator Method.)

4. $2\frac{2}{3}$ _____

5. $5\frac{1}{8}$ _____

6. $4\frac{9}{10}$ _____

7. Circle the numbers that can be rounded to 6.
(Hint: Use either the Number Line Method or the Numerator-Denominator Method.)

    a. $4\frac{5}{8}$ b. $6\frac{2}{5}$ c. $5\frac{8}{10}$

8. Circle the numbers that can be rounded to 9.
(Hint: Use either the Number Line Method or the Numerator-Denominator Method.)

    a. $8\frac{1}{4}$ b. $8\frac{4}{5}$ c. $9\frac{6}{10}$

Solve.

9. Margo measured $3\frac{5}{6}$ cups of water for the recipe to make her favorite soup. About how many cups of water did she measure? Round the mixed number to the nearest whole number.
(Hint: Use either the Number Line Method or the Numerator-Denominator Method.)

_____

Exercises on Your Own

Use this number line to help round these mixed numbers to the nearest whole number.

1. $2\frac{3}{4}$ _____

2. $7\frac{1}{4}$ _____

3. $3\frac{3}{4}$ _____

4. $5\frac{1}{4}$ _____

Round each mixed number to the nearest whole number.

5. $6\frac{1}{7}$ _____

6. $25\frac{5}{6}$ _____

7. $18\frac{3}{9}$ _____

8. $1\frac{4}{16}$ _____

9. Check the mixed number(s) that can be rounded to 7.

   a. ☐ $4\frac{6}{7}$

   b. ☐ $7\frac{2}{7}$

   c. ☐ $7\frac{5}{7}$

10. Check the mixed number(s) that can be rounded to 43.

    a. ☐ $44\frac{1}{11}$

    b. ☐ $42\frac{7}{10}$

    c. ☐ $43\frac{1}{100}$

Solve.

11. Mack weighed $75\frac{3}{4}$ pounds a week ago. This week he weighs $72\frac{1}{4}$ pounds. To estimate how much weight he lost, he first rounded the two weights to the nearest whole number. Then he did his math. Figuring this way, about how many pounds did he lose?

    _____

3.5 Review

Identify each fraction as less than 1, greater than 1, or equal to 1.

1. $\frac{2}{3}$ ___ greater than 1

___ less than 1

___ equal to 1

2. $\frac{5}{4}$ ___ greater than 1

___ less than 1

___ equal to 1

3. $\frac{7}{6}$ ___ greater than 1

___ less than 1

___ equal to 1

4. $\frac{12}{12}$ ___ greater than 1

___ less than 1

___ equal to 1

5. $\frac{3}{5}$ ___ greater than 1

___ less than 1

___ equal to 1

6. $\frac{8}{3}$ ___ greater than 1

___ less than 1

___ equal to 1

Compare these fractions by writing <, =, or > in the blank.

7. $\frac{5}{6}$ ___ $\frac{6}{5}$

8. $\frac{9}{10}$ ___ $\frac{7}{7}$

9. $\frac{5}{6}$ ___ $\frac{7}{6}$

Write these fractions in order from least to greatest.

10. $\frac{3}{4}$, $\frac{7}{6}$, $\frac{8}{8}$

_____

11. $\frac{8}{7}$, $\frac{3}{3}$, $\frac{2}{5}$

_____

12. $\frac{23}{24}$, $\frac{25}{24}$, $\frac{24}{24}$

_____

Identify each number as a fraction, a whole number, or a mixed number.

13. $4\frac{5}{7}$ ___ fraction

___ whole number

___ mixed number

14. $\frac{9}{3}$ ___ fraction

___ whole number

___ mixed number

15. 8 ___ fraction

___ whole number

___ mixed number

16. $\frac{3}{5}$ ___ fraction

___ whole number

___ mixed number

17. $1\frac{1}{6}$ ___ fraction

___ whole number

___ mixed number

3.5 REVIEW

Write mixed numbers for each of these:

18. five and two-ninths

_____

19. eighteen and seven-eighths

_____

Order these numbers from least to greatest.

20. $5\frac{2}{5}, \frac{3}{5}, \frac{7}{7}$

_____

21. $\frac{5}{5}, \frac{2}{9}, 1\frac{1}{2}$

_____

All of these fractions are greater than 1. Which ones are equivalent to whole numbers? Check *yes* or *no.*

22. $\frac{25}{5}$ ___ yes ___ no

23. $\frac{30}{4}$ ___ yes ___ no

24. $\frac{42}{6}$ ___ yes ___ no

Change each of these fractions greater than 1 to a mixed number.

25. $\frac{6}{4}$ _____

26. $\frac{13}{3}$ _____

27. $\frac{11}{2}$ _____

28. $\frac{44}{5}$ _____

Use this number line to help round these mixed numbers to the nearest whole number.

29. $3\frac{1}{3}$ _____

30. $5\frac{2}{3}$ _____

Round each mixed number to the nearest whole number.

31. $8\frac{1}{6}$ _____

32. $10\frac{5}{6}$ _____

33. $25\frac{2}{7}$ _____

Check the mixed number(s) that round to 5 when you round to the nearest whole number.

34. ☐ $5\frac{4}{5}$

35. ☐ $4\frac{7}{8}$

36. ☐ $5\frac{1}{10}$

Solve.

37. Solly lifted $125\frac{1}{4}$ pounds on Friday and $134\frac{3}{4}$ pounds on Saturday. Estimate how much more he lifted on Saturday by rounding each weight to the nearest whole number and subtracting.

_____

3. MIXED NUMBERS

38. Margo drank $8\frac{7}{8}$ cups of water after a race. Sally drank $6\frac{1}{8}$ cups. About how many more cups did Margo drink? (Round each number to the nearest whole number.)

_____

39. Billie took $\frac{5}{4}$ hours to finish hanging up some pictures. Write a mixed number for this time.

_____

40. Paula finished the interview in $\frac{5}{6}$ of an hour. Is this less than hour or more than an hour?

_____

41. Carmen typed for $\frac{9}{10}$ of an hour and Doug typed for $\frac{11}{10}$ of an hour. Who typed longer, Carmen or Doug?

_____

4. Least Common Denominator

4.1 Multiples

In Chapter 2 of this book, you learned how to find equivalent fractions. You multiplied both the numerator and denominator of a fraction by the same number.

In this lesson, you will work some more with multiplying numbers. What you learn will help you later in the chapter, when you compare fractions with different numerators and denominators.

Carl counts the number of cans of juice in 9 six-packs.

There are 6 cans in each six-pack.

Here is how Carl counts: 6, 12, 18, 24 . . . and so forth.

The numbers 6, 12, 18, 24, and so forth are called the **multiples** of 6.

You can also find the multiples of a number by multiplying.

Here is how you find the first 9 multiples of 6:

1 × 6 = **6**	4 × 6 = **24**	7 × 6 = **42**
2 × 6 = **12**	5 × 6 = **30**	8 × 6 = **48**
3 × 6 = **18**	6 × 6 = **36**	9 × 6 = **54**

There are 54 cans in 9 six-packs.

A number—like 12, for example—can be a multiple of more than one number.

Here is why.

Multiples of 2: 2, 4, 6, 8, 10, **12**   **Multiples of 6:**   6, **12**, 18, 24, 30, 36

Multiples of 3: 3, 6, 9, **12**, 15, 18   **Multiples of 12:** **12**, 24, 36, 48, 60, 72

Multiples of 4: 4, 8, **12**, 16, 20, 24

4. LEAST COMMON DENOMINATOR

12 is on all these lists. So 12 is a multiple of 2, 3, 4, 6, and 12.

EXAMPLES

There are two ways to find the first 5 multiples of 7:

1. You can multiply:

$$1 \times 7 = 7$$
$$2 \times 7 = 14$$
$$3 \times 7 = 21$$
$$4 \times 7 = 28$$
$$5 \times 7 = 35$$

2. Or you can start with 7 and add 7. And keep on adding:

$$7 \quad 7 + 7 = 14, \quad 14 + 7 = 21, \quad 21 + 7 = 28, \quad 28 + 7 = 35 \ldots$$

Either way, the first 5 multiples of 7 are 7, 14, 21, 28, 35.

We say that the number 21 is a multiple of 7.

We can turn this statement around and say that 7 is a factor of 21.

Multiples and factors are opposites. Remember:

21 is a **multiple** of 7.

7 is a **factor** of 21.

EXAMPLES

3. 24 is a multiple of 6. This means that 6 divides 24 evenly.

4. 9 divides 72 evenly. This means that 72 is a multiple of 9.

Exercises with Hints

Find the first **5** multiples of the following numbers. *(Hint: Use one of the two methods: multiply by 1, then 2, etc., or start with the number and add the number.)*

1. 2: _____

2. 5: _____

3. 10: _____

4. 9: _____

5. 4: _____

15 a multiple of several numbers. Which of these is it a multiple of? Put a check mark before each one. *(Hint: Make a list of multiples for each number. Second hint: there are 3 correct answers.)*

6. ☐ 2

7. ☐ 3

8. ☐ 4

9. ☐ 5

10. ☐ 15

Solve.

11. Jimmy was using vans to transport 58 high school students to a basketball game. Each van holds 8 passengers. Will all the vans be filled? How do you know?

   a. Yes, since 58 is a multiple of 8.

   b. Yes, since 58 is not a multiple of 8.

   c. No, since 58 is a multiple of 8.

   d. No, since 58 is not a multiple of 8.

Exercises on Your Own

Find the first **6** multiples of:

1. 9: _____

2. 8: _____

3. 11: _____

4. 100: _____

5. 25: _____

Answer **true (T)** or **false (F).**

6. 30 is a multiple of 4. _____

7. 92 is a multiple of 4. _____

8. 60 is a multiple of 5. _____

9. 8 divides 40 is the same as

   40 divides 8. _____

10. The statement "42 is a multiple of 7" is the same as "7 divides 42 evenly."

   _____

11. The statement "35 is a multiple of 5" is the same as "5 is a multiple of 35."

   _____

Solve. Check the best answer.

12. Gloria works in a large hardware store, where she is in charge of window displays. In one display there is a 36-inch space. Gloria wants to fill up the 36 inches with either a line of hammers (each 7 inches long) or a line of flashlights (each 6 inches long). After thinking, she knows she can display the flashlights this way but not the hammers. How does she know this?

   a. ☐ 6 is a multiple of 36, but 7 is not.

   b. ☐ 36 is a multiple of 6, but it is not a multiple of 7.

   c. ☐ 36 does divide 6 and does not divide 7.

4.2 Using Multiples to Find a Common Denominator

Back in *Lesson 3* of Chapter 1, you learned how to compare two fractions that have the same denominator.

In this lesson, you will learn how you can compare pairs of fractions when one of the denominators is a multiple of the other.

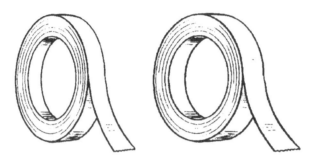

Jan works in the mail room of a large company. She uses two sizes of tape for sealing packages. One size is $\frac{3}{4}$ inch wide and the other is $\frac{7}{8}$ inch wide. Which tape is wider?

You must find which fraction is greater, $\frac{3}{4}$ or $\frac{7}{8}$.

To compare fractions, it helps if they have the same denominator (called a **common denominator**—remember?). Then you just compare numerators. (You learned this in *Lesson 1.3*.)

So to compare fractions with different denominators, you change them into equivalent fractions that have the same denominator—a common denominator.

How do you find a common denominator for the two fractions? Look at this rule:

RULE for finding a common denominator:

> *If one denominator is a **multiple** of another, then it is a **common denominator** for both of them.*

Look at the denominators of the two fractions again: $\frac{3}{\mathbf{4}}$ and $\frac{7}{\mathbf{8}}$.

    8 is a multiple of 4, so 8 is a **common denominator** for 4 and 8.

So to find out which tape is wider, $\frac{3}{4}$ inch or $\frac{7}{8}$ inch, you first change $\frac{3}{4}$ to an equivalent fraction in eighths. (If you need to, go back to *Lesson 2.4* and reread Rule 1.)

$$\frac{3}{4} = \frac{?}{8}$$

- Divide the larger denominator by the smaller:

$$8 \div 4 = 2$$

- Then multiply the answer times the numerator:

$$2 \times 3 = 6$$

$$\frac{3}{4} = \frac{6}{8}$$

$\frac{3}{4}$ and $\frac{6}{8}$ are equivalent fractions.

Now you can compare the fractions $\frac{6}{8}$ and $\frac{7}{8}$.

$$\frac{7}{8} > \frac{6}{8} \quad \text{or} \quad \frac{7}{8} > \frac{3}{4}$$

The $\frac{7}{8}$-inch tape is wider.

EXAMPLE

Which is greater, $\frac{2}{5}$ or $\frac{3}{10}$?

10 is a multiple of 5, so 10 is a common denominator for 5 and 10.

- Change $\frac{2}{5}$ to tenths by using Rule 1 of *Lesson 2.4:*

$$\frac{2}{5} = \frac{?}{10}$$

- Divide: $10 \div 5 = 2$, then multiply: $2 \times 2 = 4$

$$\frac{2}{5} = \frac{4}{10}$$

$\frac{4}{10}$ is equivalent to $\frac{2}{5}$.

Since $4 > 2$, then $\frac{4}{10} > \frac{3}{10}$.

So $\frac{2}{5} > \frac{3}{10}$.

4. LEAST COMMON DENOMINATOR

Exercises with Hints

Put a check mark in front of each exercise in which the second number is a multiple of the first number.
(Hint: Ask: Can I multiply the first number by some whole number and get the second number?)

1. ☐ 7, 42

2. ☐ 5, 34

3. ☐ 6, 24

4. ☐ 8, 46

5. ☐ 10, 40

For each pair of fractions in Exercises 6-9, which denominator can be a common denominator? Write the common denominator on the line.
(Hint: Ask: which denominator is a multiple of the other denominator?)

6. $\frac{2}{3}$, $\frac{4}{9}$ _____

7. $\frac{5}{6}$, $\frac{1}{3}$ _____

8. $\frac{7}{8}$, $\frac{5}{24}$ _____

9. $\frac{4}{5}$, $\frac{3}{20}$ _____

In Exercises 10-14, check each pair of fractions that have a denominator that can be a **common** denominator and write the common denominator on the line. (If neither fraction has a denominator that can be a common denominator, leave everything blank.)
(Hint: Look at the denominators of each pair and ask if one denominator is a multiple of the other.)

10. ☐ $\frac{3}{4}$, $\frac{4}{5}$ _____

11. ☐ $\frac{2}{5}$, $\frac{7}{30}$ _____

12. ☐ $\frac{3}{8}$, $\frac{7}{24}$ _____

13. ☐ $\frac{5}{12}$, $\frac{7}{18}$ _____

14. ☐ $\frac{1}{25}$, $\frac{79}{100}$ _____

Solve.

15. Ken worked $\frac{2}{5}$ of a day overtime last week and $\frac{3}{10}$ of a day overtime this week. In which week did he work more overtime?
(Hint: Change $\frac{2}{5}$ into an equivalent fraction that has the same denominator as $\frac{3}{10}$. Then compare the fractions.)

_____

76

4.2 USING MULTIPLES TO FIND A COMMON DENOMINATOR

Exercises on Your Own

For each pair of fractions, which denominator can be a common denominator?

1. $\frac{4}{7}$, $\frac{5}{21}$ _____

2. $\frac{3}{4}$, $\frac{5}{36}$ _____

3. $\frac{1}{2}$, $\frac{7}{50}$ _____

4. $\frac{1}{6}$, $\frac{11}{30}$ _____

Which pairs of fractions have a denominator that can be a common denominator? Write the common denominator on the line. (If there is no common denominator, leave the line blank.)

5. $\frac{5}{7}$, $\frac{3}{21}$ _____

6. $\frac{83}{90}$, $\frac{1}{10}$ _____

7. $\frac{4}{25}$, $\frac{3}{10}$ _____

8. $\frac{3}{45}$, $\frac{1}{9}$ _____

9. $\frac{9}{24}$, $\frac{7}{16}$ _____

Compare these fractions by finding a common denominator. Write the greater fraction on the line.

10. $\frac{2}{3}$, $\frac{5}{6}$ _____

11. $\frac{1}{7}$, $\frac{3}{14}$ _____

12. $\frac{3}{5}$, $\frac{7}{10}$ _____

13. $\frac{3}{8}$, $\frac{10}{24}$ _____

Which denominator of each set of fractions can be a common denominator? Write it on the line.

14. $\frac{1}{2}$, $\frac{5}{6}$, $\frac{1}{30}$ _____

15. $\frac{3}{8}$, $\frac{1}{4}$, $\frac{5}{24}$ _____

16. $\frac{3}{5}$, $\frac{2}{25}$, $\frac{24}{25}$ _____

Check each set of fractions in which one of the denominators is a common denominator.

17. ☐ $\frac{4}{9}$, $\frac{5}{18}$, $\frac{1}{2}$

18. ☐ $\frac{7}{15}$, $\frac{3}{5}$, $\frac{11}{20}$

19. ☐ $\frac{6}{14}$, $\frac{3}{7}$, $\frac{1}{4}$

20. ☐ $\frac{5}{32}$, $\frac{1}{8}$, $\frac{15}{16}$

Solve.

21. Arturo read $\frac{3}{8}$ of a book. Holly read $\frac{1}{4}$ of the same book. Who read more, Arturo or Holly?

_____

22. Sam mowed $\frac{1}{5}$ of his lawn. His sister Carla mowed $\frac{3}{10}$ of the lawn. Who mowed more, Sam or Carla?

_____

23. A convenience store is $\frac{3}{8}$ of a mile from Jones' house and $\frac{5}{16}$ of a mile from Smith's house. Who lives closer to the convenience store?

_____

4.3 Least Common Multiple (LCM)

A number that is a multiple of two other numbers is called a **common multiple** of the two numbers.

Understanding common multiples is important when you work with fractions. As you will see, they are also important in solving some unusual kinds of problems.

Jim and Kattie both work in a light bulb factory. Their job is to inspect light bulbs to see if they work.

    Jim inspects every 5th bulb.

    Kattie inspects every 6th bulb.

What number bulb will be the first bulb that they both inspect?

- Jim inspects every 5th bulb. So he inspects the following light bulbs:

  5, 10, 15, 20, 25, 30, 35, 40, 45, 50, 55, 60, 65, and so forth.

  These numbers are the *multiples* of 5.

- Kattie inspects every 6th bulb. So she inspects these light bulbs:

  6, 12, 18, 24, 30, 36, 42, 48, 54, 60, and so forth.

  These numbers are the *multiples* of 6.

The first bulb they both inspect is the first number that is on <u>both</u> lists.

Or, to put it another way, find the first multiple of 5 that is also a multiple of 6.

    Do you see that 30 is the first number that is common to <u>both</u> lists of multiples?

The first bulb they <u>both</u> inspect is the 30th, or bulb number 30.

30 is called the **least common multiple** of 5 and 6.

The abbreviation for least common multiple is **LCM**.

4.3 LEAST COMMON MULTIPLE (LCM)

EXAMPLE

To find the LCM (least common multiple) of 8 and 10, list the multiples of each number:

Multiples of 8:   8, 16, 24, 32, 40, 48, 56, 64, 72, 80

Multiples of 10:   10, 20, 30, 40, 50, 60, 70, 80, 90, 100

Find the smallest number that is common to both lists.
That number is the LCM.

In the example, 40 is the smallest number on both lists.

So 40 is the LCM (least common multiple).

Exercises with Hints

Write the first 10 multiples of each number. *(Hint: Multiply the number by 1, then 2, then 3, etc.)*

1. 7 _____

2. 9 _____

3. 3 _____

4. 12 _____

5. 5 _____

Find the LCM (least common multiple) of each pair of numbers.
(Hint: Find the multiples of one number; then the multiples of the other number. Find the first number that is on both lists.)

6. 3, 5 _____

_____

LCM: _____

7. 8, 12 _____

_____

LCM: _____

8. 15, 20 _____

_____

LCM: _____

9. 6, 7 _____

_____

LCM: _____

10. 10, 1000 _____

_____

LCM: _____

Solve.

11. There were 40 games on the basketball schedule for the Pirates. Suki played in every fourth game and Kitty played in every third game. What is the first game in which they played together?
(Hint: List the first five multiples of each number (4 and 3), then find the first number common to both lists.)

_____

_____

79

4. LEAST COMMON DENOMINATOR

12. Tara and Brian inspect the caps on bottles of soft drinks after the bottling process is completed. Tara inspects every 6th bottle and Brian inspects every 7th bottle. What is the first bottle they both inspect?

(Hint: List the first 8 multiples of each number (6 and 7), then find the first number common to both lists.)

_____

_____

Exercises on Your Own

Find the LCM of each pair of numbers.

1. 7, 8 _____

_____

LCM: _____

2. 8, 18 _____

_____

LCM: _____

3. 14, 42 _____

_____

LCM: _____

4. 3, 11 _____

_____

LCM: _____

5. 3, 25 _____

_____

LCM: _____

6. If 15 is the least common multiple of two numbers, what are the numbers? (other than 1 and 15)

_____ and _____

7. If 22 is the least common multiple of two numbers, what are the numbers? (other than 1 and 22)

_____ and _____

8. 42 is the least common multiple of these pairs (not including 1 and 42):

a. _____ and _____

b. _____ and _____

c. _____ and _____

9. 30 is the least common multiple of several pairs of numbers (not including 1 and 30). Check the pairs for which 30 is the LCM.

a. 5 and 6 _____

b. 5 and 10 _____

c. 3 and 10 _____

d. 4 and 10 _____

e. 2 and 15 _____

f. 2 and 20 _____

Solve.

10. Kal inspects every 7th flashlight battery and Olga inspects every 8th battery. Which battery will be the first one they both inspect?

_____

11. Twin robots named Marge and Al test flashlights in the factory. Marge tests every 5th flashlight and Al tests every 9th flashlight. Which flashlight will be the first one they both will test?

_____

4.4 Least Common Denominator (LCD)

You have learned how to compare fractions with the same denominator, like $\frac{3}{7}$ and $\frac{5}{7}$. You have also learned how to compare fractions when one has a denominator that is a multiple of the other, like $\frac{1}{4}$ and $\frac{3}{8}$.

In this lesson you will learn how to compare fractions with denominators that are not multiples of each other, like $\frac{2}{3}$ and $\frac{3}{5}$.

Juan wanted a wild-looking room. He painted $\frac{1}{3}$ of his room green, and $\frac{1}{4}$ of his room blue.

Is there more green than blue in Juan's room?

There are two ways to compare these fractions.

METHOD 1.

We can use the method you learned in *Lesson 1.4*. Since the fractions $\frac{1}{3}$ and $\frac{1}{4}$ have the same numerator, the fraction with the smaller denominator is greater.

Compare denominators: 4 > 3.

So $\frac{1}{4} < \frac{1}{3}$.

METHOD 2.

We can compare two fractions by finding a common denominator. This method works even when the numerators are not the same.

What is the common denominator of 4 and 3? 4 is not a multiple of 3, so 4 is not a common denominator.

> Find the least common multiple (LCM) of 3 and 4 to find the common denominator of 3 and 4. (*Remember*—common denominators are the same thing as common multiples of the denominators.)

4. LEAST COMMON DENOMINATOR

- First list the multiples of both denominators and find the least common multiple:

  Multiples of 3: 3, 6, 9, 12, 15, 18, 21, 24, and so forth.

  Multiples of 4: 4, 8, 12, 16, 20, 24, 28, 32, and so forth.

  Least common multiple: 12

  (It's the first number found on both lists of multiples.)

12 is a common denominator for the denominators 3 and 4.

12 is the *smallest* number that can be a denominator for both 3 and 4.

We call 12 the **least common denominator (LCD)** of 3 and 4.

- Now change the two fractions to equivalent fractions with the denominator 12:

  Change $\frac{1}{4}$ to twelfths.

  $$\frac{1}{4} = \frac{?}{12}$$

- Divide the larger denominator by the smaller:

  $$12 \div 4 = 3$$

- Multiply the given numerator by the answer, 3:

  $$1 \times 3 = 3$$

So $\frac{1}{4} = \frac{3}{12}$

- Now change $\frac{1}{3}$ to twelfths:

  $$\frac{1}{3} = \frac{?}{12}$$

- Divide denominators:

  $$12 \div 3 = 4$$

- Multiply the given numerator by the answer, 4:

  $$4 \times 1 = 4$$

So $\frac{1}{3} = \frac{4}{12}$

Now you can answer the question.

- Compare: $\frac{4}{12} > \frac{3}{12}$

Therefore, $\frac{1}{3} > \frac{1}{4}$

There is more green than blue in Gary's room.

EXAMPLE

Which is greater, $\frac{2}{3}$ or $\frac{3}{5}$?

In this example the numerators are different, so we cannot use the method of *Lesson 1.4.* We use the method of finding the LCD (least common denominator).

Use the LCM of 3 and 5 to find the LCD of 3 and 5.

Multiples of 3: 3, 6, 9, 12, 15, 18, 21, 24, 27, 30

Multiples of 5: 5, 10, 15, 20, 25, 30, 35, 40, 45, 50

The LCM of 3 and 5 is 15, so the LCD (least common denominator) is 15.

- Change both fractions to their equivalents with the denominator 15:

$$\frac{2}{3} = \frac{?}{15}$$

- Divide: $15 \div 3 = 5$; multiply: $5 \times 2 = 10$

$$\frac{2}{3} = \frac{10}{15}$$

- Now change $\frac{3}{5}$ to its equivalent with the denominator 15:

$$\frac{3}{5} = \frac{?}{15}$$

- Divide: $15 \div 5 = 3$; multiply: $3 \times 3 = 9$

$$\frac{3}{5} = \frac{9}{15}$$

- Compare: $\frac{10}{15} > \frac{9}{15}$.

Therefore, $\frac{2}{3} > \frac{3}{5}$.

4. LEAST COMMON DENOMINATOR

Exercises with Hints

Find the LCM's of these pairs.
(Hint: Find the multiples of each number, then find the least common multiple.)

1. 7, 14 _____

_____

LCM: _____

2. 4, 18 _____

_____

LCM: _____

3. 6, 36 _____

_____

LCM: _____

4. 8, 12 _____

_____

LCM: _____

5. 5, 7 _____

_____

LCM: _____

Find the LCD of these fractions. *(Hint: Find the LCM's of the denominators.)*

6. $\frac{2}{5}$ and $\frac{1}{2}$ _____

_____

LCD: _____

7. $\frac{1}{6}$ and $\frac{5}{12}$ _____

_____

LCD: _____

8. $\frac{2}{3}$ and $\frac{7}{8}$ _____

_____

LCD: _____

In Exercises 9 and 10, use the LCD to find which is greater.
(Hint: Follow the steps in the Example before the Exercises.)

9. Which is greater, $\frac{4}{5}$ or $\frac{7}{9}$? _____

10. Which is greater, $\frac{4}{5}$ or $\frac{1}{2}$? _____

In Exercises 11 and 12, use either Method 1 or 2 above to find which is greater.
(Hint: The numerators are the same in both exercises.)

11. $\frac{1}{5}$ or $\frac{1}{3}$ _____

12. $\frac{4}{7}$ or $\frac{4}{9}$ _____

Solve.

13. Pat and Alex both work part time. Pat works $\frac{2}{3}$ of a full time job, and Alex works $\frac{3}{5}$ of a full time job. Who works longer, Pat or Alex?
(Hint: Compare the fractions by finding the LCD.)

_____

4.4 LEAST COMMON DENOMINATOR (LCD)

Exercises on Your Own

Find the LCD for these fractions.

1. $\frac{4}{5}$ and $\frac{2}{9}$

_____

2. $\frac{5}{6}$ and $\frac{3}{4}$

_____

3. $\frac{1}{3}$ and $\frac{7}{8}$

_____

4. $\frac{1}{2}$ and $\frac{4}{5}$

_____

5. $\frac{6}{7}$ and $\frac{3}{4}$

_____

6. $\frac{1}{12}$ and $\frac{2}{3}$

_____

7. $\frac{3}{10}$ and $\frac{1}{4}$

_____

8. $\frac{1}{2}$ and $\frac{5}{6}$

_____

9. $\frac{5}{6}$ and $\frac{3}{5}$

_____

In Exercises 10-13, find which is greater.

10. $\frac{4}{7}$ or $\frac{3}{5}$ _____

11. $\frac{5}{8}$ or $\frac{5}{7}$ _____

12. $\frac{3}{5}$ or $\frac{1}{2}$ _____

13. $\frac{3}{7}$ or $\frac{3}{5}$ _____

Solve.

14. Edan removed snow from his side-walk for $\frac{5}{6}$ of an hour. Curt removed snow from his car for $\frac{4}{5}$ of an hour. Who spent more time removing snow, Edan or Curt?

_____

4.5 Review

Write the first 6 multiples of:

1. 7: ___ , ___ , ___ , ___ , ___ , ___

2. 3: ___ , ___ , ___ , ___ , ___ , ___

3. 50: ___ , ___ , ___ , ___ , ___ , ___

Answer **T (true)** or **F (false)**.

4. 32 is a multiple of 4. _____

5. 36 is a multiple of 5. _____

6. 54 is a multiple of 6. _____

7. 72 is a multiple of some of these numbers. Which ones? Check them.

   a. ☐ 2

   b. ☐ 4

   c. ☐ 5

   d. ☐ 6

   e. ☐ 7

8. 100 is a multiple of some of these numbers. Which ones? Check them.

   a. ☐ 2

   b. ☐ 5

   c. ☐ 8

   d. ☐ 10

   e. ☐ 15

Do these pairs of fractions have a denominator that could be a **common** denominator? If so, write the common denominator on the line.

9. $\frac{3}{8}$, $\frac{15}{24}$ _____

10. $\frac{5}{12}$, $\frac{9}{30}$ _____

11. $\frac{4}{25}$, $\frac{1}{5}$ _____

Compare these fractions by finding a common denominator. Write **<** or **>**.

12. $\frac{5}{8}$ ___ $\frac{3}{4}$

13. $\frac{2}{3}$ ___ $\frac{5}{9}$

14. $\frac{1}{2}$ ___ $\frac{6}{10}$

15. $\frac{5}{12}$ ___ $\frac{7}{24}$

For each set of fractions, which denominator can be a common denominator? Write it on the line.

16. $\frac{2}{3}$, $\frac{6}{15}$, $\frac{1}{5}$ _____

17. $\frac{1}{24}$; $\frac{3}{8}$, $\frac{5}{12}$ _____

18. $\frac{3}{14}$, $\frac{5}{21}$, $\frac{1}{7}$ _____

Find the least common multiple of each pair of numbers.

19. 5, 7 _____

20. 3, 8 _____

21. 4, 32 _____

22. 8, 14 _____

23. 9, 12 _____

Find the LCD for these fractions.

24. $\frac{3}{7}$ and $\frac{2}{5}$ _____

25. $\frac{5}{8}$ and $\frac{3}{4}$ _____

26. $\frac{1}{9}$ and $\frac{5}{6}$ _____

27. $\frac{7}{10}$ and $\frac{1}{3}$ _____

28. $\frac{5}{12}$ and $\frac{3}{5}$ _____

Compare fractions in Exercises 29-32. Write < or >.

29. $\frac{4}{5}$ _____ $\frac{3}{7}$

30. $\frac{3}{4}$ _____ $\frac{5}{8}$

31. $\frac{3}{10}$ _____ $\frac{1}{3}$

32. $\frac{5}{8}$ _____ $\frac{5}{6}$

Solve.

33. Curt spent $\frac{3}{5}$ of an hour becoming familiar with the new program on his office computer. Janice spent $\frac{5}{6}$ of an hour becoming familiar with it. Who took longer to become familiar with the program, Curt or Janice?

_____

34. Dottie inspects every fifth computer disk in the factory. Howard inspects every ninth computer disk. Which computer disk is the first one they both inspect?

_____

35. Robin and Norma make the same salary. Robin said that $\frac{1}{3}$ of her salary was deducted for taxes. Norma said that $\frac{2}{7}$ of her salary was deducted for taxes. Who had more deducted for taxes, Robin or Norma?

_____

36. A box of Yummie-Nut Cereal is 6 inches wide, 9 inches high and 3 inches deep. Explain why it is better to ship these cereal boxes in a carton 36 inches wide, 45 inches high, and 15 inches deep, than in a carton 36 inches wide, 47 inches high, and 14 inches deep.

_____

_____

_____

_____

5. **Comparing Fractions**

5.1 Comparing Fractions

In the last chapter, you learned how to find the LCM of two numbers (or the LCD of two fractions). In this lesson, you will learn another way to find an LCM or LCD.

Raúl took a long bus trip.

He slept for $\frac{2}{5}$ of the trip and read for $\frac{3}{8}$ of the trip.

Did he sleep longer than he read?

To find the answer, we have to compare the fractions $\frac{2}{5}$ and $\frac{3}{8}$.

We do this the usual way:
- First change them into equivalent fractions with the same denominator.
- Then compare numerators.

Start by finding a number, the LCM (Lowest Common Multiple) that can be used as a common denominator for the two fractions.

There are two ways to find the LCM. We will call these **Method 1** and **Method 2.**

Both methods use multiples of the denominators.
- Method 1 uses the multiples of *both* denominators. This is the method you learned in earlier lessons.
- Method 2 is a new method for you. It uses the multiples of the larger denominator only. It's a little faster than Method 1.

5.1 COMPARING FRACTIONS

METHOD 1. *Using the Multiples of 5 and 8*

This is the method you learned in earlier lessons.

Multiples of 5: 5, 10, 15, 20, 20, 25, 30, 35, **40**, 45, and so forth.

Multiples of 8: 8, 16, 24, 32, **40**, 48, 56, 64, and so forth.

So the LCM of 5 and 8 is 40.

METHOD 2. *Using the Multiples of 8*

In this method we will use the multiples of the larger denominator. In this case, the larger denominator is 8.

Multiples of 8: 8, 16, 24, 32, 40, 48, 56, 64, and so forth.

- Check each multiple of 8, starting with 8, to see if it is the LCM.

    To do this, you check each multiple of 8 to see if 5 is a factor or not.
    That is, try to divide each multiple by 5 and see if it can be done evenly.

- As soon as you find a multiple for which 5 is a factor, then that multiple is the LCM.

    Is 5 a factor of 8?   No. 5 can't be divided into 8 evenly.

    Is 5 a factor of 16?   No. 16 isn't divisible by 5, either.

    Is 5 a factor of 24?   No.

    Is 5 a factor of 32?   No.

    Is 5 a factor of 40?   **Yes!**

Since 5 and 8 are both factors of 40, then 40 is the LCM.

And 40 is also the LCD for the fractions $\frac{2}{5}$ and $\frac{3}{8}$.

- You have found the LCD. It is 40. Now rewrite the fractions.

    Change both $\frac{2}{5}$ and $\frac{3}{8}$ to equivalent fractions with denominators of 40:

    Rewrite $\frac{2}{5}$. $\frac{2}{5} = \frac{?}{40}$

    Divide: $40 \div 5 = 8$; multiply: $8 \times 2 = 16$

    $$\frac{2}{5} = \frac{16}{40}$$

    Now rewrite $\frac{3}{8}$. $\frac{3}{8} = \frac{?}{40}$

    Divide: $40 \div 8 = 5$; multiply: $5 \times 3 = 15$

    $$\frac{3}{8} = \frac{15}{40}$$

89

5. COMPARING FRACTIONS

- Now you can answer the question.

  Compare: $\frac{16}{40} > \frac{15}{40}$

  So $\frac{2}{5} > \frac{3}{8}$

Raúl slept longer than he read on the trip.

EXAMPLE

1. Which is longer, $\frac{4}{5}$ of a yard or $\frac{3}{4}$ of a yard?

Find the LCM of the denominators:

> **METHOD 1. Use Multiples of Both Denominators**
>
> **Multiples of 5:** 5, 10, 15, **20**, 25, 30, 35, 40, and so forth.
>
> **Multiples of 4:** 4, 8, 12, 16, **20**, 24, 28, 32, and so forth.
>
> The LCM of 5 and 4 is 20.

> **METHOD 2. Use Multiples of the Larger Denominator Only**
>
> Use the multiples of the larger denominator, which is 5.
>
> **Multiples of 5:** 5, 10, 15, 20, 25, 30, 35, 40, and so forth.
>
> Check to see if 4 is a factor of each multiple (Try dividing 4 into each one.)
>
> 4 is a factor of 20, so 20 is the LCM of 5 and 4.

Using either method, we have found that the LCD for $\frac{4}{5}$ and $\frac{3}{4}$ is 20.

2. Change both $\frac{4}{5}$ and $\frac{3}{4}$ to equivalent fractions with the denominator 20:

Find the equivalent fraction of $\frac{4}{5}$. $\qquad \frac{4}{5} = \frac{?}{20}$

Divide: $20 \div 5 = 4$; multiply: $4 \times 4 = 16$

$$\frac{4}{5} = \frac{16}{20}$$

Find the equivalent fraction of $\frac{3}{4}$. $\qquad \frac{3}{4} = \frac{?}{20}$

Divide: $20 \div 4 = 5$; multiply: $5 \times 3 = 15$

$$\frac{3}{4} = \frac{15}{20}$$

Compare: $\frac{16}{20} > \frac{15}{20}$

So $\frac{4}{5} > \frac{3}{4}$

5.1 COMPARING FRACTIONS

Exercises with Hints

Find the LCM of each pair of numbers.
(Hint: Use either Method 1 or Method 2 described in this lesson.)

1. 6, 8 _____

   _____

   LCM: _____

2. 5, 9 _____

   _____

   LCM: _____

3. 10, 15 _____

   _____

   LCM: _____

Find the LCD for each pair of fractions.
(Hint: Find the LCM of each denominator. It's the same as the LCD.)

4. $\frac{1}{3}$, $\frac{3}{5}$ _____

   _____

   LCD: _____

5. $\frac{5}{8}$, $\frac{1}{6}$ _____

   _____

   LCD: _____

6. $\frac{9}{10}$, $\frac{3}{20}$ _____

   _____

   LCD: _____

Compare the fractions in each pair. Which one is greater?
(Hint: Use LCM to find the LCD, then compare fractions. Follow the steps in the examples above.)

7. $\frac{5}{6}$, $\frac{6}{7}$

   The greater fraction is _____.

8. $\frac{1}{2}$, $\frac{4}{7}$

   The greater fraction is _____.

9. $\frac{2}{15}$, $\frac{1}{6}$

   The greater fraction is _____.

Solve.

10. Monique figures that she spends about $\frac{3}{10}$ of her time at work speaking on the phone and about $\frac{2}{7}$ of the time at a computer. What does she spend more time doing, talking on the phone or working at the computer?
    (Hint: Find the LCD and compare fractions.)

    _____

    _____

5. COMPARING FRACTIONS

Exercises on Your Own _____

Find the LCD of each pair of fractions.

1. $\dfrac{4}{5}$, $\dfrac{23}{30}$ _____

2. $\dfrac{7}{9}$, $\dfrac{22}{27}$ _____

3. $\dfrac{6}{7}$, $\dfrac{4}{5}$ _____

4. $\dfrac{2}{3}$, $\dfrac{4}{15}$ _____

5. $\dfrac{7}{8}$, $\dfrac{3}{4}$ _____

6. $\dfrac{2}{11}$, $\dfrac{5}{22}$ _____

Show why each sentence is true by changing each pair of fractions into equivalent fractions with the same denominator. (Be careful of the difference between < and >!)

7. $\dfrac{2}{5} > \dfrac{3}{10}$ _____

8. $\dfrac{2}{7} > \dfrac{4}{15}$ _____

9. $\dfrac{7}{30} < \dfrac{4}{15}$ _____

Solve.

10. Bob saw $\dfrac{2}{3}$ of a movie and Greg saw $\dfrac{6}{10}$ of the same movie. Who saw more of the movie?

    _____

11. Grace read the newspaper for $\dfrac{5}{12}$ of an hour. Mary read the same newspaper for $\dfrac{1}{2}$ of an hour. Who read the paper longer?

    _____

5.2 Finding the LCD: More Than Two Fractions
(One Denominator is a Multiple of One of the Others)

Now you are ready to find the LCD of more than two fractions. In this lesson, one of the denominators is a multiple of one of the others. This makes finding the LCD of three fractions a little easier.

Jodi, Robin, and Harry started watching a movie on video.

Jodi watched $\frac{3}{4}$ of the video.

Robin watched $\frac{2}{3}$ of the video.

Harry watched $\frac{1}{2}$ of the video.

Who watched the most? Who watched the least?

To compare these the three fractions $\frac{3}{4}$, $\frac{2}{3}$, and $\frac{1}{2}$, we must find the least common denominator (LCD) of all three.

- Use the least common multiple (LCM) to find the LCD.
- Find the LCM of 2, 3, and 4.

There are two ways to find the LCM. (See *Lesson 5.1*)

METHOD 1. Using Multiples of 2, 3, and 4

4 is a multiple of 2, so the multiples of 4 are also be multiples of 2.

Multiples of 4:   4, 8, 12, 16, 20, 24, 28, 32, and so forth.

Multiples of 3:   3, 6, 9, 12, 16, 20, 24, 28, and so forth.

The LCM of 4 and 3 is 12.

The LCM of 4, 3, and 2 is 12.

5. COMPARING FRACTIONS

METHOD 2. *Using Multiples of 4*

In this method, keep checking the multiples of the largest number (4) until you find the multiple that works. (Remember, 4 is a multiple of 2, so the multiples of 4 are also multiples of 2.)

Multiples of 4: 4, 8, 12, 16, 20, 24, 28, 32, and so forth.

- Start with the smallest multiple, which is 4. See which one is also a multiple of 3.

    Is 3 a factor of 4?   No. 3 can't be divided into 4 evenly.

    Is 3 a factor of 8?   No. 8 isn't divisible by 3, either.

    Is 3 a factor of 12? Yes.

The LCD of $\frac{3}{4}$, $\frac{2}{3}$, and $\frac{1}{2}$ is 12.

- Change each fraction to an equivalent with a denominator of 12.

    To find the numerator of the equivalent fraction, first divide 12 by the denominator of the original fraction.

    Then multiply the answer by the numerator of the original fraction.

$$\frac{3}{4} = \frac{3 \times \mathbf{3}}{4 \times \mathbf{3}} = \frac{9}{12} \qquad \frac{2}{3} = \frac{2 \times \mathbf{4}}{3 \times \mathbf{4}} = \frac{8}{12} \qquad \frac{1}{2} = \frac{1 \times \mathbf{6}}{2 \times \mathbf{6}} = \frac{6}{12}$$

- Compare $\frac{9}{12}$, $\frac{8}{12}$, and $\frac{6}{12}$.

$\frac{6}{12}$ ($= \frac{1}{2}$) is the *least* of the three fractions.

$\frac{9}{12}$ ($= \frac{3}{4}$) is the *greatest* of the three fractions.

Jodi watched the most. Harry watched the least.

EXAMPLE

Place these fractions in order from the least to the greatest: $\frac{5}{7}$, $\frac{2}{3}$, and $\frac{5}{6}$.

1. To find the LCD, find the LCM of 7, 3, and 6.

METHOD 1. Use Multiples of 7, 3, and 6

Since 6 is a multiple of 3, all multiples of 6 are also multiples of 3. List the multiples of 7 and 6 only.

Multiples of 7: 7, 14, 21, 28, 35, 42, 49, 56, and so forth.

Multiples of 6: 6, 12, 18, 24, 30, 36, 42, 48, and so forth.

The LCM of 7, 3, and 6 is 42.

94

5.2 FINDING THE LCD: MORE THAN TWO FRACTIONS

METHOD 2. Using Multiples of the Largest Denominator

Start with the largest denominator and look at its multiples.

Multiples of 7:   7, 14, 21, 28, 35, 42, 49, 56, and so forth

6 is a multiple of 3. So if 6 is a factor of a number, then so is 3.

Check to find which multiple is also a multiple of 6.

6 is a factor of 42, so 42 is the LCM of 7, 6, and 3.

Using either method, we have found that the LCD for $\frac{5}{7}$, $\frac{2}{3}$, and $\frac{5}{6}$ is 42.

2. Change the fractions $\frac{5}{7}$, $\frac{2}{3}$, and $\frac{5}{6}$ to equivalent fractions with denominators of 42.

- Divide 42 by each denominator.

- Then multiply the numerator and denominator of each fraction by the quotient to get an equivalent fraction.

$$\frac{5}{7} = \frac{5 \times 6}{7 \times 6} = \frac{30}{42} \qquad \frac{2}{3} = \frac{2 \times 14}{3 \times 14} = \frac{28}{42} \qquad \frac{1}{2} = \frac{1 \times 21}{2 \times 21} = \frac{21}{42}$$

The fractions in order from the least to the greatest are $\frac{1}{2}$, $\frac{2}{3}$, and $\frac{5}{7}$.

Exercises with Hints _____

What is the LCD for each set of fractions? *(Hint: Find the LCM of the denominators.)*

1. $\frac{3}{4}$, $\frac{5}{6}$, $\frac{5}{12}$ _____

2. $\frac{1}{8}$, $\frac{3}{5}$, $\frac{9}{20}$ _____

3. $\frac{1}{2}$, $\frac{5}{6}$, $\frac{2}{3}$ _____

For Exercises 4-6, use the LCD to find equivalent fractions for each fraction of the set.
(Hint: Find the LCM of the denominators, and change each fraction to an equivalent fraction with that denominator.)

4. $\frac{1}{3}$, $\frac{5}{6}$, $\frac{7}{12}$

_____ , _____ , _____

5. $\frac{3}{5}$, $\frac{1}{10}$, $\frac{4}{15}$

_____ , _____ , _____

6. $\frac{3}{4}$, $\frac{1}{2}$, $\frac{3}{10}$

_____ , _____ , _____

5. COMPARING FRACTIONS

Answer **T (True)** or **F (False)** to Exercises 7-10. If your answer is False, then find the correct answer.
(Hint: Find the LCM of the denominators.)

7. 40 is the LCD for $\frac{1}{4}$, $\frac{2}{5}$, and $\frac{3}{10}$.

_____

8. 50 is the LCD for $\frac{3}{25}$, $\frac{1}{2}$, and $\frac{7}{10}$.

_____

9. The LCD for $\frac{1}{3}$, $\frac{3}{4}$, and $\frac{5}{6}$ is 24.

_____

10. The LCD for $\frac{5}{100}$, $\frac{3}{25}$, and $\frac{7}{10}$ is 100. _____

Solve.

11. Kerry played basketball for $\frac{3}{4}$ of an hour. Jim played for $\frac{2}{3}$ of an hour, and Nick played for $\frac{5}{6}$ of an hour. Place these times in order from smallest to largest.
(Hint: Find the LCM of the denominators and use it as the LCD.)

_____

Exercises on Your Own

What is the LCD for each set of fractions?

1. $\frac{7}{10}$, $\frac{5}{20}$, $\frac{23}{30}$ _____

2. $\frac{2}{5}$, $\frac{5}{12}$, $\frac{3}{20}$ _____

3. $\frac{3}{7}$, $\frac{1}{4}$, $\frac{5}{14}$ _____

For Exercises 4-7, use the LCD to find equivalent fractions for each fraction of the set.

4. $\frac{2}{5}$, $\frac{1}{3}$, and $\frac{7}{10}$

_____ , _____ , _____

5. $\frac{5}{6}$, $\frac{7}{12}$, and $\frac{1}{2}$

_____ , _____ , _____

6. $\frac{7}{8}$, $\frac{3}{20}$, and $\frac{4}{5}$

_____ , _____ , _____

7. $\frac{9}{10}$, $\frac{7}{20}$, and $\frac{9}{30}$

_____ , _____ , _____

Answer **T (True)** or **F (False)** to Exercises 8-10. If the answer is False, then find the correct answer.

8. The LCD for $\frac{1}{2}$, $\frac{1}{5}$, and $\frac{1}{6}$ is 30.

_____

9. The LCD for $\frac{3}{5}$, $\frac{1}{8}$, and $\frac{7}{20}$ is 20.

_____

10. The LCD for $\frac{1}{2}$, $\frac{1}{9}$, and $\frac{4}{27}$ is 27.

_____

Solve.

11. Barry said that it rained for $\frac{5}{12}$ of the day where he lived. Ethel said it rained for $\frac{3}{8}$ of the day where she lived. Greta said it rained for $\frac{1}{3}$ of the day where she lived. Where did it rain the most? Where did it rain the least?

_____

5.3 Ordering Fractions
(More Than Two Fractions)

Now you are ready to compare three fractions whose denominators are not multiples.

Kumi, Nora, and Jessie
are all reading the same book.

Kumi read $\frac{3}{5}$ of the book.

Nora read $\frac{2}{3}$ of the book.

Jessie read $\frac{1}{2}$ of the book.

Who read the most? Who read the least?

Compare $\frac{3}{5}$, $\frac{2}{3}$, and $\frac{1}{2}$ to find which is the greatest and which is the least.

To compare $\frac{3}{5}$, $\frac{2}{3}$, and $\frac{1}{2}$, find the least common multiple (LCM) of the denominators. This is the least common denominator (LCD).

None of the denominators 5, 3, and 2 is a multiple of any of the other denominators.

You can use either of the two methods introduced in *Lesson 5.1* to find the LCM.

METHOD 1. Using Multiples of 5, 3, and 2

Multiples of 5: 5, 10, 15, 20, 25, **30**, 35, 40, 45, 50, and so forth.

Multiples of 3: 3, 6, 9, 12, 15, 18, 21, 24, 27, **30**, and so forth.

Multiples of 2: 2, 4, 6, 8, 10, 12, 14, 16, 18, 20, 22, 24, 26, 28, **30**, and so forth.

The LCM of 5, 3, and 2 is 30.

METHOD 2. *Using Multiples of 5*

- Check the multiples of the largest number (5) until you find the multiple that works.

    Make a list of the multiples of 5:

    5, 10, 15, 20, 25, 30, 35, 40, 45, 50, and so forth.

    Check each multiple starting with 5 to see if it is the LCM.

    As soon as you find a multiple for which 3 and 2 are factors, then that multiple is the LCM.

    Start with 5.

    Are 2 and 3 factors of 5? No, neither is.

    So check the next multiple of 5, which is 10.

    2 is a factor of 10, but 3 is not.

    Check the next multiple of 5, which is 15.

    3 is a factor of 15, but 2 is not.

    Keep checking the multiples of 5 until you find one for which 2 and 3 are factors.

    2 and 3 are factors of 30, so it is the LCM of 5, 3, and 2.

    The LCD of $\frac{3}{5}$, $\frac{2}{3}$, and $\frac{1}{2}$ is 30.

- Change the three fractions to equivalent fractions with a denominator of 30:

$$\frac{3}{5} = \frac{3 \times 6}{5 \times 6} = \frac{18}{30} \qquad \frac{2}{3} = \frac{2 \times 10}{3 \times 10} = \frac{20}{30} \qquad \frac{1}{2} = \frac{1 \times 15}{2 \times 15} = \frac{15}{30}$$

Now you can answer the question.

Compare: $\frac{15}{30} < \frac{18}{30} < \frac{20}{30}$

So $\frac{1}{2} < \frac{3}{5}$ and $\frac{3}{5} < \frac{2}{3}$

Jessie read the least and Nora read the most.

5.3 ORDERING FRACTIONS

EXAMPLE

Write these fractions in order from least to greatest:

$$\frac{4}{5}, \frac{3}{4}, \frac{5}{6}$$

1. Find the LCM of 5, 4, and 6. Use either Method 1 or Method 2.

    METHOD 1. Using Multiples of 5, 4, and 6

    Multiples of 5: 5, 10, 15, 20, 25, 30, 35, 40, 45, 50, 55, **60**, 65, and so forth.

    Multiples of 4: 4, 8, 12, 16, 20, 24, 28, 32, 36, 40, 44, 48, 52, 46, **60**, 64, and so forth.

    Multiples of 6: 6, 12, 18, 24, 30, 36, 42, 48, 54, **60**, 66, 72, and so forth.

    The LCM of 5, 4, and 6 is 60.

    METHOD 2. Using Multiples of 6

    Check the multiples of 6, the largest denominator, to find the first multiple for which 5 and 4 are also factors.

    Multiples of 6: 6, 12, 18, 24, 30, 36, 42, 48, 54, **60**, and so forth.

    The first multiple that works for both 4 and 5 is 60.

    5 and 4 are factors of 60, so 60 is the LCM of 4, 5, and 6.

    Using either method, we have found that the LCD of $\frac{4}{5}$, $\frac{3}{4}$, and $\frac{5}{6}$ is 60.

2. Change the fractions to equivalent fractions with a denominator of 60:

    $$\frac{4}{5} = \frac{4 \times \mathbf{12}}{5 \times \mathbf{12}} = \frac{48}{60} \qquad \frac{3}{4} = \frac{3 \times \mathbf{15}}{4 \times \mathbf{15}} = \frac{45}{60} \qquad \frac{5}{6} = \frac{5 \times \mathbf{10}}{6 \times \mathbf{10}} = \frac{50}{60}$$

    Compare. Remember, the question asks for the order from *least* to *greatest*:

    $$\frac{45}{60} < \frac{48}{60} < \frac{50}{60}$$

    So $\frac{3}{4} < \frac{4}{5} < \frac{5}{6}$.

    The order of the fractions from the least to the greatest is $\frac{3}{4}$, $\frac{4}{5}$, and $\frac{5}{6}$.

5. COMPARING FRACTIONS

Exercises with Hints

Find the LCM of each set of numbers.
(Hint: Use either Method 1 or Method 2.)

1. 4, 5, 6   LCM: _____

2. 2, 3, 5   LCM: _____

3. 3, 5, 7   LCM: _____

Find the LCD for each set of fractions.
(Hint: Find the LCM by using Method 1 or Method 2.)

4. $\frac{3}{4}$, $\frac{1}{6}$, $\frac{5}{12}$ LCD: _____

5. $\frac{1}{2}$, $\frac{4}{5}$, $\frac{7}{8}$ LCD: _____

6. $\frac{3}{10}$, $\frac{1}{12}$, $\frac{7}{15}$ LCD: _____

In Exercises 7-10, write the fractions in order from least to greatest.
(Hint: First, write equivalent fractions using the LCD. Follow one of the methods in the Example before the Exercises.)

7. $\frac{6}{7}$, $\frac{3}{5}$, $\frac{7}{10}$ _____

8. $\frac{4}{5}$, $\frac{5}{8}$, $\frac{11}{12}$ _____

9. $\frac{2}{3}$, $\frac{5}{6}$, $\frac{7}{12}$ _____

10. $\frac{4}{5}$, $\frac{6}{7}$, $\frac{2}{3}$ _____

Solve.

11. Anita spent $\frac{1}{5}$ of her money on the movies. She spent $\frac{2}{7}$ of her money on food and $\frac{3}{10}$ of her money on videos. On which item did she spend the most? On which item did she spend the least?
(Hint: Find the LCM of the denominators. Then find the equivalent fractions with the LCD, and compare.)

_____

_____

100

Exercises on Your Own

Find the LCD for each set of fractions.

1. $\dfrac{1}{6}$, $\dfrac{5}{12}$, $\dfrac{7}{24}$ _____

2. $\dfrac{6}{7}$, $\dfrac{9}{14}$, $\dfrac{25}{42}$ _____

3. $\dfrac{3}{100}$, $\dfrac{7}{10}$, $\dfrac{27}{50}$ _____

4. $\dfrac{4}{9}$, $\dfrac{5}{18}$, $\dfrac{3}{4}$ _____

Write these fractions in order from least to greatest.

5. $\dfrac{2}{5}$, $\dfrac{3}{7}$, $\dfrac{17}{35}$ _____

6. $\dfrac{5}{8}$, $\dfrac{3}{4}$, $\dfrac{7}{12}$ _____

7. $\dfrac{1}{6}$, $\dfrac{3}{10}$, $\dfrac{4}{15}$ _____

8. $\dfrac{5}{8}$, $\dfrac{1}{2}$, $\dfrac{7}{12}$ _____

9. $\dfrac{3}{10}$, $\dfrac{3}{5}$, $\dfrac{5}{9}$ _____

10. $\dfrac{7}{50}$, $\dfrac{3}{25}$, $\dfrac{1}{5}$ _____

Solve.

11. Smith, Jones and Brown all have the same project to do. Smith completed $\dfrac{5}{6}$ of the project. Jones completed $\dfrac{7}{10}$, and Brown finished $\dfrac{7}{8}$ of the project.

   a. Who finished the most?

   _____

   b. Who finished the least?

   _____

5.4 Comparing and Ordering Mixed Numbers

If you know how to compare fractions, you'll have no trouble comparing mixed numbers.

Jim is fixing the plumbing in his house.
He needs three pipes:

- one $4\frac{1}{4}$ feet long,
- a second one $4\frac{3}{8}$ feet long,
- and a third one $3\frac{1}{2}$ feet long.

Which pipe is the shortest?

Which pipe is the longest?

The numbers $4\frac{1}{4}$, $4\frac{3}{8}$, and $3\frac{1}{2}$ are mixed numbers.

To compare mixed numbers, compare the **whole number** parts first.

Since $3 < 4$, $3\frac{1}{2}$ is the least of the three numbers. The shortest pipe is $3\frac{1}{2}$ feet long.

To compare mixed numbers that have the same whole number part, compare the fractional parts.

To compare $4\frac{1}{4}$ and $4\frac{3}{8}$, just compare $\frac{1}{4}$ and $\frac{3}{8}$.

Use 8 as a least common denominator (LCD):

$$\frac{1}{4} = \frac{1 \times \mathbf{2}}{4 \times \mathbf{2}} = \frac{2}{8}$$

Compare: $\frac{3}{8} > \frac{2}{8}$

So $4\frac{3}{8} > 4\frac{1}{4}$

The longest pipe is $4\frac{3}{8}$ feet long.

5.4 COMPARING AND ORDERING MIXED NUMBERS

EXAMPLE

Write the mixed numbers $2\frac{5}{8}$, $2\frac{2}{3}$, and $2\frac{7}{12}$ in order from least to greatest.

The whole number part for all three mixed numbers is 2.

So, we compare the fractional parts $\frac{5}{8}$, $\frac{2}{3}$, and $\frac{7}{12}$.

Find the LCD for the denominators.

The least common multiple (LCM) of 8, 3, and 12 is 24.

So the LCD for $\frac{5}{8}$, $\frac{2}{3}$, and $\frac{7}{12}$ is 24.

$$\frac{5}{8} = \frac{5 \times 3}{8 \times 3} = \frac{15}{24} \qquad \frac{2}{3} = \frac{2 \times 8}{3 \times 8} = \frac{16}{24} \qquad \frac{7}{12} = \frac{7 \times 2}{12 \times 2} = \frac{14}{24}$$

The fractions in order are $\frac{14}{24}$, $\frac{15}{24}$, and $\frac{16}{24}$.

So the original fractions, in order, are $\frac{7}{12}$, $\frac{5}{8}$, and $\frac{2}{3}$.

And the mixed numbers, in order, are $2\frac{7}{12}$, $2\frac{5}{8}$, and $2\frac{2}{3}$.

Exercises with Hints

Write these mixed numbers in order from the least to the greatest.
(Hint: Compare the whole numbers parts.)

1. $7\frac{3}{5}$, $6\frac{3}{7}$, $5\frac{7}{9}$

_____

2. $43\frac{1}{5}$, $44\frac{2}{13}$, $42\frac{5}{43}$

_____

Find the greater mixed number.
(Hint: Since the whole number parts are the same, find the LCD and compare fractional parts.)

3. $6\frac{2}{3}$, $6\frac{4}{7}$ _____

4. $6\frac{8}{9}$, $6\frac{5}{6}$ _____

5. $2\frac{9}{10}$, $2\frac{4}{5}$ _____

Write these mixed numbers in order from least to greatest.
(Hint: Check the whole number parts first, then compare fractional parts.)

6. $1\frac{4}{5}$, $1\frac{6}{7}$, $2\frac{2}{7}$

_____

7. $3\frac{1}{2}$, $3\frac{3}{8}$, $3\frac{5}{8}$

_____

8. $20\frac{5}{6}$, $21\frac{5}{6}$, $21\frac{11}{12}$

_____

103

5. COMPARING FRACTIONS

9. $45\frac{2}{7}$, $46\frac{1}{7}$, $42\frac{4}{7}$

_____

Solve.

10. Mike, Henry, and Roland use the same recipe to bake a cake, but they use different amounts of flour. Mike uses $2\frac{2}{3}$ cups, Henry uses $2\frac{2}{5}$ cups, and Roland uses $2\frac{1}{2}$ cups.

Who uses the most? Who uses the least?

(Hint: Since the whole number parts of all the numbers are the same, compare the fractional parts.)

_____

_____

Exercises on Your Own

Write these mixed numbers in order from the least to the greatest.

1. $4\frac{4}{5}$, $5\frac{2}{7}$, $3\frac{8}{9}$

_____

2. $70\frac{5}{8}$, $75\frac{3}{4}$, $73\frac{11}{12}$

_____

Find the greater mixed number.

3. $5\frac{2}{5}$, $5\frac{3}{10}$ _____

4. $7\frac{5}{6}$, $7\frac{17}{18}$ _____

5. $3\frac{2}{9}$, $3\frac{5}{18}$ _____

Write these mixed numbers in order from least to greatest.

6. $2\frac{5}{8}$, $1\frac{7}{8}$, $1\frac{5}{8}$

_____

7. $8\frac{2}{13}$, $8\frac{5}{13}$, $8\frac{7}{13}$

_____

8. $10\frac{1}{10}$, $10\frac{3}{5}$, $10\frac{2}{25}$

_____

9. $1\frac{3}{5}$, $1\frac{4}{15}$, $1\frac{7}{30}$

_____

Solve.

10. Juan measured the heights of the four cabinets in his kitchen. They were $2\frac{1}{2}$ feet, $2\frac{3}{4}$ feet, $2\frac{5}{12}$ feet, and $2\frac{11}{12}$ feet.

a. Which height is the smallest?

_____

b. Which is the greatest?

_____

5.5 Review

Find the LCD of each pair of fractions.

1. $\frac{3}{4}$, $\frac{7}{20}$ _____

2. $\frac{1}{9}$, $\frac{20}{27}$ _____

3. $\frac{3}{5}$, $\frac{2}{3}$ _____

4. $\frac{7}{10}$, $\frac{5}{6}$ _____

5. $\frac{5}{12}$, $\frac{1}{4}$ _____

6. $\frac{8}{15}$, $\frac{4}{9}$ _____

Write <, =, or > to compare each pair of fractions.

7. $\frac{3}{5}$ ___ $\frac{7}{10}$

8. $\frac{23}{30}$ ___ $\frac{11}{15}$

9. $\frac{3}{5}$ ___ $\frac{3}{4}$

10. $\frac{1}{6}$ ___ $\frac{2}{11}$

11. $\frac{5}{8}$ ___ $\frac{11}{20}$

12. $\frac{1}{2}$ ___ $\frac{7}{18}$

What is the LCD for each set of fractions?

13. $\frac{2}{5}$, $\frac{3}{20}$, $\frac{9}{10}$ _____

14. $\frac{3}{8}$, $\frac{4}{5}$, $\frac{7}{20}$ _____

15. $\frac{3}{4}$, $\frac{8}{9}$, $\frac{17}{18}$ _____

For Exercises 16-19, use the LCD to find equivalent fractions for each fraction of the set.

16. $\frac{4}{5}$, $\frac{7}{20}$, $\frac{1}{4}$

_____ , _____ , _____

17. $\frac{2}{3}$, $\frac{7}{12}$, $\frac{1}{6}$

_____ , _____ , _____

18. $\frac{3}{40}$, $\frac{7}{8}$, $\frac{13}{20}$

_____ , _____ , _____

19. $\frac{7}{9}$, $\frac{7}{18}$, $\frac{20}{27}$

_____ , _____ , _____

Write these fractions in order from least to greatest.

20. $\frac{4}{7}$, $\frac{11}{21}$, $\frac{1}{3}$

_____

21. $\frac{3}{8}$, $\frac{5}{12}$, $\frac{1}{2}$

_____

22. $\frac{4}{5}$, $\frac{19}{25}$, $\frac{29}{50}$

_____

23. $\frac{5}{6}$, $\frac{11}{12}$, $\frac{43}{48}$

_____

24. $\frac{7}{8}$, $\frac{4}{9}$, $\frac{3}{4}$

_____

5. COMPARING FRACTIONS

Find the greater mixed number.

25. $7\frac{2}{3}$, $7\frac{5}{6}$ _____

26. $12\frac{1}{5}$, $12\frac{2}{9}$ _____

27. $1\frac{3}{7}$, $1\frac{5}{14}$ _____

Write these mixed numbers in order from the least to the greatest.

28. $5\frac{2}{5}$, $5\frac{14}{25}$, $5\frac{3}{10}$

_____

29. $3\frac{3}{11}$, $3\frac{5}{22}$, $3\frac{10}{33}$

_____

30. $10\frac{1}{2}$, $10\frac{1}{3}$, $10\frac{1}{4}$

_____

Solve.

31. Coretta spent $\frac{2}{3}$ hour trying to fix her VCR. Felicia spent $\frac{3}{4}$ hour fixing her computer. Who spent more time fixing equipment, Coretta or Felicia?

_____

32. Harry spoke on the telephone for $\frac{3}{4}$ of an hour, Karen spoke for $\frac{5}{6}$ of an hour, and Florence spoke for $\frac{4}{5}$ of an hour.

a. Who spoke the most? _____

b. Who spoke the least? _____

33. Carlos is $5\frac{7}{8}$ feet tall. Mario is $5\frac{3}{4}$ feet tall. Who is taller, Carlos or Mario?

_____

34. The three longest jumps in the broad jump event were $8\frac{3}{10}$ meters, $8\frac{2}{5}$ meters, and $8\frac{23}{100}$ meters.

a. Which was the longest jump?

_____

b. Which was the shortest jump?

_____

6. Adding Fractions

6.1 Estimating Sums and Differences

You have already learned nearly everything you need to know in order to add and subtract fractions and mixed numbers. This lesson is like a warm-up. You will learn how to **estimate** the sums and differences of mixed numbers before you learn how to do actual addition and subtraction.

Maggie has two boards she wants to use to build a bookcase.

The boards are $2\frac{3}{4}$ feet and $4\frac{1}{8}$ feet long.

Estimate how long they are altogether.

To **estimate** the sum of the lengths, round each length to the nearest foot.

$2\frac{3}{4}$ feet is closer to 3 feet than to 2 feet.

So, $2\frac{3}{4}$ **rounded** to the nearest whole numbers is 3.

$4\frac{1}{8}$ feet is closer to 4 feet than to 5 feet.

So, $4\frac{1}{8}$ **rounded** to the nearest whole number is 4.

To estimate the sum: $2\frac{3}{4} + 4\frac{1}{8}$, use the rounded numbers:

$$3 + 4 = 7$$

The length of the two boards is about 7 feet.

107

6. ADDING FRACTIONS

RULE *for estimating the sum or difference of two mixed numbers:*

> **Round each mixed number to the nearest whole number. Then add the whole numbers.**

EXAMPLE

Estimate the difference: $9\frac{4}{5} - 5\frac{1}{6} = ?$

1. Round each mixed number to the nearest whole number:

$9\frac{4}{5}$ —— rounds to ——> 10

$5\frac{1}{6}$ —— rounds to ——> 5

2. Subtract the whole numbers: $10 - 5 = 5$ (the estimate)

Exercises with Hints

Round each mixed number to the nearest whole number.
(Hint: Which whole number is the mixed number closest to?)

1. $15\frac{1}{7}$ _____

2. $6\frac{8}{9}$ _____

3. $40\frac{2}{7}$ _____

4. $59\frac{9}{10}$ _____

Estimate each sum.
(Hint: Round each mixed number to the nearest whole number. Then add the whole numbers.)

5. $4\frac{1}{5} + 1\frac{5}{6} =$ about _____

6. $7\frac{7}{8} + 5\frac{4}{5} =$ about _____

7. $2\frac{6}{7} + 9\frac{3}{20} =$ about _____

8. $30\frac{4}{25} + 40\frac{7}{10} =$ about _____

9. $6\frac{2}{9} + 4\frac{1}{10} =$ about _____

10. $1\frac{3}{40} + 2\frac{4}{23} =$ about _____

Solve.

11. Max needs three boards $4\frac{5}{6}$ feet long each. About how long will the three boards be altogether?
(Hint: Round the length to the nearest whole number. Then add three whole numbers.)

_____

6.1 ESTIMATING SUMS AND DIFFERENCES

12. Coretta spent $1\frac{3}{4}$ hours on the phone selling her company's products, then she spent $3\frac{4}{5}$ hours at her computer writing. About how much more time was she at the computer than on the phone?

(Hint: Round the mixed numbers to the nearest whole number. Then subtract the whole numbers.)

_____

Exercises on Your Own

Round each mixed number to the nearest whole number.

1. $2\frac{1}{4}$ _____

2. $4\frac{6}{7}$ _____

3. $90\frac{2}{15}$ _____

4. $8\frac{5}{6}$ _____

Estimate each sum.

5. $7\frac{1}{6} + 3\frac{2}{11} =$ about _____

6. $1\frac{7}{8} + 3\frac{11}{12} =$ about _____

7. $7\frac{1}{10} + 7\frac{9}{10} =$ about _____

8. $40\frac{3}{10} + 20\frac{9}{13} =$ about _____

9. $5\frac{5}{28} + 6\frac{7}{32} =$ about _____

10. $2\frac{4}{45} + 10\frac{1}{8} =$ about _____

Solve.

11. Julie exercised for $2\frac{1}{5}$ hours, then rested for $1\frac{3}{4}$ hours. About how long did she exercise and rest?

_____

12. Mavis sang in the choir for $2\frac{3}{4}$ hours in the morning and for $1\frac{1}{6}$ hours in the afternoon. About how long did she sing altogether?

_____

13. The football field that Lenno practices on is $83\frac{2}{3}$ yards long and $43\frac{1}{3}$ yards wide. Estimate how much longer the length is than the width.

_____

109

6.2 Adding Fractions with Like Denominators

The easiest fractions to add are fractions with the same denominator. All you do is add numerators. This lesson will show you how.

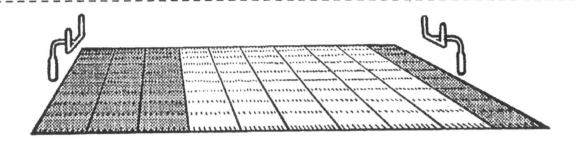

Marty and Hans have the job of mowing the football field at school.

Marty mowed $\frac{3}{10}$ of the field.

Hans mowed $\frac{1}{10}$ of the field.

How much of the field did they mow together?

To find the answer, add:

$$\frac{3}{10} + \frac{1}{10} = ?$$

These fractions have the same denominators, sometimes called **like denominators.** (In math, the word *like* often means "the same" or "similar.")

Use the diagram of the football field to add these fractions:

$$\frac{3}{10} + \frac{1}{10} = \frac{4}{10}$$

Simplify the answer:

$$\frac{4}{10} = \frac{4 \div \mathbf{2}}{10 \div \mathbf{2}} = \frac{2}{5}$$

Marty and Hans mowed $\frac{2}{5}$ of the football field.

6.2 ADDING FRACTIONS WITH LIKE DENOMINATORS

RULE: *How to add two fractions with like denominators:*

1. *Make sure the denominators of the fractions are* <u>*like*</u> *denominators.*

2. *Add the numerators.*

3. *The sum of the fractions is this fraction:*

   Sum of the numerators
   ────────────────────
   Like denominator

4. *Simplify the answer.*

EXAMPLE

Add: $\dfrac{5}{14} + \dfrac{3}{14} = ?$

1. The denominators are *like* denominators. Both are 14.

2. The sum of the numerators is $5 + 3 = 8$.

3. The sum of the two fractions is—

$$\frac{5+3}{14} = \frac{8}{14}$$

4. Simplify the answer:

$$\frac{8}{14} = \frac{8 \div \mathbf{2}}{14 \div \mathbf{2}} = \frac{4}{7}$$

The answer is $\dfrac{4}{7}$.

Exercises with Hints

Put a check mark before each pair of fractions that have like denominators.
(Hint: Two denominators are "like" if they are the same.)

1. ☐ $\dfrac{2}{7}$, $\dfrac{5}{7}$

2. ☐ $\dfrac{4}{11}$, $\dfrac{3}{11}$

3. ☐ $\dfrac{9}{13}$, $\dfrac{13}{14}$

Which fractions have been added correctly? Put a check mark before them.
(Hint: Check to see if the denominators are like and the numerators are added correctly.)

4. ☐ $\dfrac{2}{5} + \dfrac{1}{5} = \dfrac{3}{5}$

5. ☐ $\dfrac{7}{15} + \dfrac{3}{13} = \dfrac{10}{15}$

6. ☐ $\dfrac{5}{9} + \dfrac{1}{9} = \dfrac{6}{9}$

6. ADDING FRACTIONS

7. ☐ $\dfrac{5}{8} + \dfrac{3}{10} = \dfrac{5}{10}$

8. ☐ $\dfrac{7}{100} + \dfrac{21}{100} = \dfrac{26}{100}$

9. ☐ $\dfrac{2}{9} + \dfrac{2}{9} = \dfrac{4}{9}$

Add the fractions. Simplify the answers.
(Hint: If the denominators are like denominators, then add the numerators.)

10. $\dfrac{1}{7} + \dfrac{3}{7} = $ _____

11. $\dfrac{2}{9} + \dfrac{3}{9} = $ _____

12. $\dfrac{5}{21} + \dfrac{4}{21} = $ _____

13. $\dfrac{5}{49} + \dfrac{9}{49} = $ _____

Solve.

14. Luisa works in a shoe store. Last Thursday she inspected $\dfrac{1}{7}$ of a shipment and last Friday she inspected $\dfrac{4}{7}$ of the same shipment. What part of the shipment did she inspect altogether on these two days?
(Hint: Use the rule before the example.)

_____

Exercises on Your Own

Put a check mark before each set of fractions that has been added correctly.

1. ☐ $\dfrac{4}{15} + \dfrac{2}{15} = \dfrac{6}{15}$

2. ☐ $\dfrac{9}{17} + \dfrac{3}{16} = \dfrac{12}{17}$

3. ☐ $\dfrac{7}{9} + \dfrac{1}{9} = \dfrac{8}{9}$

4. ☐ $\dfrac{7}{13} + \dfrac{5}{13} = \dfrac{13}{13}$

Add the fractions. Simplify the answers.

5. $\dfrac{7}{30} + \dfrac{7}{30} = $ _____

6. $\dfrac{7}{12} + \dfrac{1}{12} = $ _____

7. $\dfrac{13}{20} + \dfrac{7}{20} = $ _____

8. $\dfrac{1}{8} + \dfrac{3}{8} = $ _____

9. $\dfrac{14}{15} + \dfrac{1}{15} = $ _____

10. $\dfrac{6}{23} + \dfrac{5}{23} = $ _____

Solve.

11. Joe had a book report to write. He did $\dfrac{1}{3}$ of the report on Monday and $\dfrac{1}{3}$ of the report on Tuesday.

  a. How much of his report did he get done? _____

  b. How much more does he have to do? _____

  (This is subtraction. But you should be able to figure out how to do it!)

12. Vanessa slept $\dfrac{3}{8}$ of the day and studied $\dfrac{1}{8}$ of the day. What total part of the day did she sleep and study? *(Remember to simplify!)*

_____

6.3 Adding Fractions with Unlike Denominators

You have learned how to add fractions with the same (like) denominators. How do you add fractions with different denominators? You change them to equivalent fractions that have like denominators, then add. This lesson will give you practice.

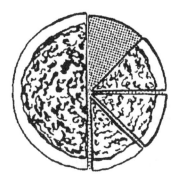

Willie ate $\frac{1}{2}$ of this pizza, and Greg ate $\frac{3}{8}$ of the pizza.

How much did they eat altogether?

$$\frac{1}{2} + \frac{3}{8} = ?$$

You can't just add the numerators. The fractions have different denominators, called **unlike denominators.**

- To add these fractions, first find the least common denominator (LCD) of 2 and 8.
  Since 8 is a multiple of 2, 8 is the LCD.

- Change $\frac{1}{2}$ to eighths in the usual way:

   Divide the denominators: $8 \div 2 = 4$

   Multiply your answer times the numerator: $4 \times 1 = 4$

So $\frac{1}{2} = \frac{4}{8}$

$\frac{1}{2}$ and $\frac{4}{8}$ are equivalent fractions. So you can use $\frac{4}{8}$ for $\frac{1}{2}$.

Now you have two fractions with like denominators: $\frac{4}{8}$ and $\frac{3}{8}$.

---

6. ADDING FRACTIONS

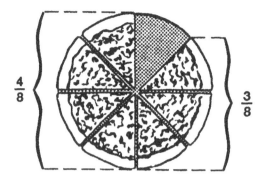

Use the diagram to add.

To find the sum, add the numerators:

$$\frac{4}{8} + \frac{3}{8} = \frac{7}{8}$$

Together, Willie and Greg ate $\frac{7}{8}$ of the pizza.

RULE: *How to add two fractions with unlike denominators:*

---

1. **Find the LCD.**
2. **Change the fractions to equivalent fractions with like denominators.**
3. **Add the numerators.**
4. **Simplify the answer.**

EXAMPLE

Add: $\frac{3}{5} + \frac{1}{6} = ?$

Use the Rule:

1. Find the LCD.

    The LCD is the least common multiple (LCM) of 5 and 6.

    The LCM of 5 and 6 is 30.

2. Change the fractions to fractions with like denominators.

    Change $\frac{3}{5}$ to an equivalent fraction in 30ths:

    Divide denominators: $30 \div 5 = 6$

    Multiply the answer times the numerator: $6 \times 3 = 18$

    So $\frac{3}{5} = \frac{18}{30}$

Change $\frac{1}{6}$ to an equivalent fraction in 30ths:

Divide denominators: $30 \div 6 = 5$

Multiply the answer times the numerator: $5 \times 1 = 5$

So $\frac{1}{6} = \frac{5}{30}$

3. Add the numerators.

$$\frac{18}{30} + \frac{5}{30} = \frac{23}{30}$$

4. The answer is already simplified.

Exercises with Hints

Find the LCD of each pair of fractions.
(Hint: Use the LCM.)

1. $\frac{3}{4}$, $\frac{3}{16}$ _____

2. $\frac{4}{9}$, $\frac{1}{4}$ _____

3. $\frac{3}{7}$, $\frac{1}{2}$ _____

Here are the same pairs of fractions you just worked with. Use the results of Exercises 1-3 to change the fractions to fractions with like denominators.
(Hint: Use methods for finding equivalent fractions.)

4. $\frac{3}{4}$, $\frac{3}{16}$ _____

5. $\frac{4}{9}$, $\frac{1}{4}$ _____

6. $\frac{3}{7}$, $\frac{1}{2}$ _____

Use the results of Exercises 4-6 to add these fractions. Simplify if you can.
(Hint: The denominators are like, so you can now add the numerators.)

7. $\frac{3}{4} + \frac{3}{16} =$ _____

8. $\frac{4}{9} + \frac{1}{4} =$ _____

9. $\frac{3}{7} + \frac{1}{2} =$ _____

Solve.

10. Dwight calculated that he spends $\frac{2}{7}$ of his monthly income on food and $\frac{1}{5}$ on rent. What fraction of his monthly income does he spend on food and rent?
(Hint: Follow the steps of the rule in this chapter.)

_____

6. ADDING FRACTIONS

Exercises on Your Own

Find the LCD of each set of fractions. (Do not add them yet).

1. $\dfrac{5}{6}$, $\dfrac{7}{30}$ _____

2. $\dfrac{3}{8}$, $\dfrac{2}{5}$ _____

3. $\dfrac{1}{4}$, $\dfrac{2}{7}$ _____

In Exercises 4-6, use the results of Exercises 1-3 to change the fractions to fractions with like denominators. Do not add.

4. $\dfrac{5}{6}$, $\dfrac{7}{30}$ _____

5. $\dfrac{3}{8}$, $\dfrac{2}{5}$ _____

6. $\dfrac{1}{4}$, $\dfrac{2}{7}$ _____

For Exercises 7-9, use the results of Exercises 4-6 to add these fractions. Simplify if you can.

7. $\dfrac{5}{6}$ + $\dfrac{7}{30}$ = _____

8. $\dfrac{3}{8}$ + $\dfrac{2}{5}$ = _____

9. $\dfrac{1}{4}$ + $\dfrac{2}{7}$ = _____

Solve.

10. Carmen drank $\dfrac{1}{8}$ gallon of juice before the game and $\dfrac{1}{4}$ gallon of juice after the game. What part of a gallon did Carmen drink altogether? (Don't forget to simplify—if you can.)

_____

11. Stan played first base for $\dfrac{1}{9}$ of the game and center field for $\dfrac{1}{3}$ of the game. What fraction of the game did he play?

_____

116

6.4 Adding Mixed Numbers

When you add mixed numbers, you first add the whole number parts, then add the fraction parts. Finally, you combine the two.

It's not difficult. However, there is one type of problem that you should look out for. You'll meet it in Example 2.

Don worked $4\frac{3}{5}$ hours on figuring out his taxes. After a short break, he worked another $2\frac{1}{5}$ hours. How many hours did he work on his taxes?

To find the answer, add:

$$4\frac{3}{5} + 2\frac{1}{5} = ?$$

To add two mixed numbers, write the mixed numbers under each other:

$$\begin{array}{r} 4\frac{3}{5} \\ +\ 2\frac{1}{5} \\ \hline ? \end{array}$$

Add the whole number parts and the fraction parts separately:

$$\begin{array}{r} 4 \\ +\ 2 \\ \hline 6 \end{array} \qquad \begin{array}{r} \frac{3}{5} \\ +\ \frac{1}{5} \\ \hline \frac{4}{5} \end{array}$$

$6\frac{4}{5}$ cannot be simplified.

Don worked $6\frac{4}{5}$ hours on his taxes.

117

6. ADDING FRACTIONS

RULE: *How to add two mixed numbers:*

1. *Write the mixed numbers under each other.*

2. *Add the whole numbers.*

3. *Add the fractions.*

4. *Simplify the sum.*

EXAMPLE 1

Add: $5\dfrac{1}{5} + 7\dfrac{2}{3}$

1. Write the mixed numbers under each other.

$$\begin{array}{r} 5\dfrac{1}{5} \\ +\ 7\dfrac{2}{3} \\ \hline \end{array}$$

2. Add the whole numbers.

$$\begin{array}{r} 5\dfrac{1}{5} \\ +\ 7\dfrac{2}{3} \\ \hline 12\ldots \end{array}$$

3. Add the fractions. Find the LCD and change the fractions.

$$\begin{array}{r} 5\dfrac{1}{5} \\ +\ 7\dfrac{2}{3} \\ \hline 12\ldots \end{array} \longrightarrow \begin{array}{r} 5\dfrac{3}{15} \\ +\ 7\dfrac{10}{15} \\ \hline 12\dfrac{13}{15} \end{array}$$

4. Simplify the sum if you can.

The answer $12\dfrac{13}{15}$ is in simplest form.

EXAMPLE 2

Add: $4\dfrac{3}{4} + \dfrac{15}{8} = \ ?$

The fraction $\dfrac{15}{8}$ is greater than 1, so change it to a mixed number:

$$\frac{15}{8} = 1\frac{7}{8}$$

1. Write the mixed numbers under each other:

$$\begin{array}{r} 4\dfrac{3}{4} \\ +\ 1\dfrac{7}{8} \\ \hline \end{array}$$

118

6.4 ADDING MIXED NUMBERS

2. Add the whole numbers.

$$4\frac{3}{4}$$
$$+\ 1\frac{7}{8}$$
$$\overline{\quad 5\ldots}$$

3. Add the fractions. Find the LCD, change the fractions, and add.

$$4\frac{3}{4} \longrightarrow 4\frac{6}{8}$$
$$+\ 1\frac{7}{8} \longrightarrow +\ 1\frac{7}{8}$$
$$\overline{\quad 5\ldots} \longrightarrow \overline{\quad 5\frac{13}{8}}$$

4. Simplify the sum if you can.

$$\frac{13}{8} = 1\frac{5}{8}$$

So, $5\frac{13}{8} = 5 + 1\frac{5}{8} = 6\frac{5}{8}$

The sum is $6\frac{5}{8}$.

Exercises with Hints

Put a check mark before each exercise that asks for the sum of two mixed numbers.
(Hint: A mixed number is made up of a whole number part and a fraction part.)

1. ☐ $\quad 4\frac{2}{5} + 2\frac{3}{4}$

2. ☐ $\quad \frac{6}{13} + 10\frac{2}{7}$

3. ☐ $\quad 6\frac{1}{2} + \frac{1}{2}$

4. ☐ $\quad 1\frac{7}{8} + 21\frac{5}{6}$

Put a check mark before each exercise where you have to find the LCD to solve the problem.
(Hint: Look for unlike denominators.)

5. ☐ $\quad 5\frac{1}{7} + 3\frac{3}{7}$

6. ☐ $\quad 2\frac{1}{8} + 3\frac{1}{27}$

7. ☐ $\quad \frac{5}{6} + 12\frac{6}{7}$

8. ☐ $\quad 9\frac{1}{9} + 7\frac{2}{9}$

Add the mixed numbers. Remember to simplify if you need to.
(Hint: Use the 4 steps of the rule.)

9. $4\frac{2}{11} + 8\frac{7}{11} =$ _____

10. $20\frac{5}{12} + 8\frac{5}{12} =$ _____

11. $5\frac{3}{8} + 8\frac{1}{3} =$ _____

12. $7\frac{3}{5} + 2\frac{7}{15} =$ _____

119

6. ADDING FRACTIONS

Solve.

13. Chuck brought two boxes to the Post Office. One weighed $6\frac{4}{5}$ pounds and the other weighs $5\frac{1}{2}$ pounds.

How much did the two boxes weigh together?

(Hint: Use the 4 steps in Example 1.)

_____

Exercises on Your Own

Put a check mark before each exercise where you have to find the LCD to solve the problem.

1. ☐ $10\frac{3}{20} + 5\frac{1}{10} = ?$

2. ☐ $9\frac{2}{17} + 8\frac{1}{17} = ?$

3. ☐ $40\frac{7}{10} + 10\frac{1}{10} = ?$

4. ☐ $8\frac{5}{8} + 3\frac{1}{4} = ?$

Add the mixed numbers. Remember to simplify if you can.

5. $1\frac{1}{9} + 2\frac{4}{9} =$ _____

6. $10\frac{4}{5} + 20\frac{3}{5} =$ _____

7. $2\frac{5}{12} + 7\frac{1}{6} =$ _____

8. $5\frac{3}{8} + 8\frac{2}{3} =$ _____

9. $8\frac{5}{7} + 8\frac{5}{6} =$ _____

10. $3\frac{3}{10} + 12\frac{23}{30} =$ _____

Solve.

11. Harry rowed $4\frac{5}{6}$ miles downstream and $2\frac{5}{8}$ miles upstream. How far did he row altogether?

_____

12. Janet worked at the computer for $5\frac{2}{5}$ hours on Monday and for $6\frac{1}{6}$ hours on Tuesday. How long did she work at the computer in those two days?

_____

120

6.5 Review

Round each mixed number to the nearest whole number.

1. $4\frac{4}{5}$ _____

2. $12\frac{1}{3}$ _____

3. $80\frac{12}{17}$ _____

4. $11\frac{2}{5}$ _____

Estimate each sum.

5. $3\frac{1}{5} + 7\frac{2}{9} =$ _____

6. $14\frac{5}{6} + 10\frac{2}{7} =$ _____

7. $8\frac{7}{8} + 9\frac{3}{5} =$ _____

8. $20\frac{3}{10} + 30\frac{3}{11} =$ _____

Add the fractions.

9. $\frac{2}{7} + \frac{3}{7} =$ _____

10. $\frac{4}{11} + \frac{5}{11} =$ _____

11. $\frac{1}{9} + \frac{4}{9} =$ _____

12. $\frac{8}{17} + \frac{5}{17} =$ _____

Find the LCD of each set of fractions. Do not add.

13. $\frac{3}{5} + \frac{3}{10} =$ **?** LCD: _____

14. $\frac{2}{7} + \frac{9}{14} =$ **?** LCD: _____

15. $\frac{4}{15} + \frac{1}{2} =$ **?** LCD: _____

16. $\frac{3}{8} + \frac{1}{3} =$ **?** LCD: _____

In Exercises 17-20, use the LCD's of Exercises 13-16 to change the fractions to fractions with like denominators. Do not add.

17. $\frac{3}{5} + \frac{3}{10} =$ **?** _____ + _____ = **?**

18. $\frac{2}{7} + \frac{9}{14} =$ **?** _____ + _____ = **?**

19. $\frac{4}{15} + \frac{1}{2} =$ **?** _____ + _____ = **?**

20. $\frac{3}{8} + \frac{1}{3} =$ **?** _____ + _____ = **?**

For Exercises 21-24, use the results of Exercises 17-20 to add these fractions.

21. $\frac{3}{5} + \frac{3}{10} =$ _____

22. $\frac{2}{7} + \frac{9}{14} =$ _____

23. $\frac{4}{15} + \frac{1}{2} =$ _____

24. $\frac{3}{8} + \frac{1}{3} =$ _____

6. ADDING FRACTIONS

Add the mixed numbers. Simplify if you need to.

25. $7\frac{1}{8} + 2\frac{3}{8} = $ _____

26. $4\frac{5}{9} + 2\frac{5}{18} = $ _____

27. $13\frac{5}{12} + 7\frac{1}{6} = $ _____

28. $9\frac{4}{5} + 8\frac{3}{4} = $ _____

29. $15\frac{2}{3} + 9\frac{8}{9} = $ _____

Solve.

30. Clarence said he drove for $4\frac{2}{5}$ hours. About how long did he drive? *(Round to the nearest whole number.)*

_____

31. James played in a football game on Saturday morning. It lasted $3\frac{1}{4}$ hours. Then he played soccer for $1\frac{2}{3}$ hours. Estimate the total amount of hours he played football and soccer. *(Round to the nearest whole number.)*

_____

32. Lorenzo exercised for $\frac{2}{5}$ of an hour, and rested. Then he exercised for another $\frac{2}{5}$ of an hour. What fraction of an hour did he exercise altogether?

_____

33. To make a shelf in her office, Emilia placed two boards end-to-end. One board was $\frac{3}{4}$ foot and the other was $\frac{2}{3}$ of a foot. How long are the boards together?

_____

34. Linda studies for $2\frac{3}{5}$ hours in the morning and $1\frac{3}{10}$ hour in the afternoon. How long did she study altogether?

_____

35. Cora drove $15\frac{2}{5}$ miles to the mall and another $12\frac{7}{8}$ miles to the movies. What was the total distance she drove?

_____

36. Pedro placed 3 tiles end-to-end. Each tile was $8\frac{3}{4}$ inches long. How long will the 3 tiles be together?

_____

37. Paul drank $3\frac{3}{4}$ glasses of water after a race. Three hours later, he drank $2\frac{2}{3}$ glasses of water. How much water did he drink altogether?

_____

7. Subtracting Fractions

7.1 Subtracting Fractions with Like Denominators

When you subtract fractions that have the same denominators (like denominators), you just subtract the numerators. This lesson will give you practice.

Jackie lives $\frac{7}{8}$ mile from the movie theater.

Carla lives $\frac{1}{8}$ of a mile from the movie theater.

How much further away from the movie house is Jackie than Carla?

To find the answer, subtract:

$$\frac{7}{8} - \frac{1}{8} = ?$$

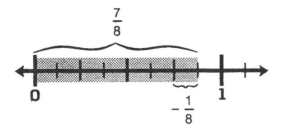

These fractions have the same denominators, called **like denominators.**

Use the diagram to subtract the fractions:

$$\frac{7}{8} - \frac{1}{8} = \frac{6}{8}$$

Reduce $\frac{6}{8}$ to simplest form:

$$\frac{6}{8} = \frac{6 \div \mathbf{2}}{8 \div \mathbf{2}} = \frac{3}{4}$$

Jackie is $\frac{3}{4}$ mile further away from the movie house than Carla.

---

7. SUBTRACTING FRACTIONS

RULE: *How to subtract fractions with like denominators:*

1. *Make sure the denominators of the fractions are <u>like</u> denominators.*

2. *Subtract the numerators.*

3. *The difference of the fractions is this fraction:*

$$\frac{\text{Difference of the numerators}}{\text{Like denominator}}$$

4. *Simplify the answer if you can.*

EXAMPLE

Subtract: $\frac{13}{15} - \frac{7}{15}$

1. The denominators are like denominators—both are 15.

2. Subtract the numerators: $13 - 7 = 6$.

3. The difference is this fraction:

$$\frac{13}{15} - \frac{7}{15} = \frac{6}{15}$$

4. Simplify the difference:

$$\frac{6}{15} = \frac{6 \div \mathbf{3}}{15 \div \mathbf{3}} = \frac{2}{5}$$

The answer is $\frac{2}{5}$.

Exercises with Hints

Put a check mark before each exercise that shows fractions with like denominators.
(Hint: Rermember—two denominators are "like" if they are exactly the same.)

1. ☐ $\frac{4}{7} - \frac{2}{7}$

2. ☐ $\frac{9}{11} - \frac{3}{11}$

3. ☐ $\frac{9}{13} - \frac{3}{14}$

Put a check mark before each exercise where the fractions have been subtracted correctly.
(Hint: Look for 2 things. See if the denominators are like and see if the numerators have been subtracted correctly.)

4. ☐ $\frac{2}{5} - \frac{1}{5} = \frac{1}{5}$

5. ☐ $\frac{7}{15} - \frac{3}{13} = \frac{4}{15}$

6. ☐ $\frac{5}{9} - \frac{1}{9} = \frac{6}{9}$

7.1 SUBTRACTING FRACTIONS WITH LIKE DENOMINATORS

7. ☐ $\dfrac{5}{8} - \dfrac{3}{10} = \dfrac{2}{10}$

8. ☐ $\dfrac{17}{100} - \dfrac{7}{100} = \dfrac{10}{17}$

9. ☐ $\dfrac{2}{9} - \dfrac{2}{9} = 1$

Subtract the fractions.
(Hint: If the denominators are like denominators, then subtract the numerators.)

10. $\dfrac{6}{7} - \dfrac{3}{7} =$ _____

11. $\dfrac{7}{9} - \dfrac{3}{9} =$ _____

12. $\dfrac{17}{21} - \dfrac{4}{21} =$ _____

13. $\dfrac{15}{49} - \dfrac{9}{49} =$ _____

Solve.

14. Saretha bought a board $\dfrac{5}{6}$ ft. long. She then cut $\dfrac{1}{6}$ foot off the board to make a shelf for her office. How long is the shelf?
(Hint: Don't forget to simplify!)

_____

Exercises on Your Own

Put a check mark before each exercise where the fractions have been subtracted correctly.

1. ☐ $\dfrac{4}{7} - \dfrac{1}{7} = \dfrac{3}{7}$

2. ☐ $\dfrac{7}{17} - \dfrac{6}{17} = \dfrac{1}{7}$

3. ☐ $\dfrac{2}{9} - \dfrac{1}{9} = \dfrac{1}{9}$

4. ☐ $\dfrac{13}{20} - \dfrac{3}{20} = \dfrac{1}{2}$

5. ☐ $\dfrac{9}{10} - \dfrac{7}{10} = \dfrac{1}{5}$

6. ☐ $\dfrac{22}{25} - \dfrac{4}{25} = \dfrac{19}{25}$

Subtract the fractions.

7. $\dfrac{9}{11} - \dfrac{2}{11} =$ _____

8. $\dfrac{14}{15} - \dfrac{1}{15} =$ _____

9. $\dfrac{17}{22} - \dfrac{8}{22} =$ _____

10. $\dfrac{3}{8} - \dfrac{3}{8} =$ _____

Solve.

11. John ran $\dfrac{7}{8}$ of a mile and walked $\dfrac{3}{8}$ of a mile. How much further did he run than walk?

_____

12. Carol is $\dfrac{11}{12}$ inches taller than her sister Ruby and $\dfrac{5}{12}$ inches taller than her brother Randy. How much taller is Randy than Ruby?

_____

7.2 Subtracting Fractions with Unlike Denominators

When you subtract fractions with different (unlike) denominators, you first change one or both into equivalent fractions with the same (like) denominators. Then you subtract numerators.

As you will see, you follow the same basic steps that you do in addition—only you are subtracting.

Mary used $\frac{5}{6}$ gallon of paint

to paint her room.

She used $\frac{1}{3}$ gallon of red paint.

The rest was blue.

How much blue paint did she use?

To find the answer, subtract:

$$\frac{5}{6} - \frac{1}{3} = ?$$

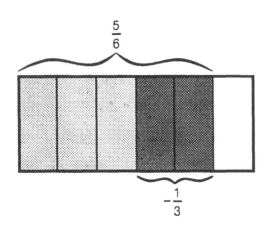

These fractions do not have the same denominators. The denominators are unlike.

Change the fractions to fractions with like denominators.

Since 6 is a multiple of 3 change $\frac{1}{3}$ to sixths:

$$\frac{1}{3} = \frac{1 \times \mathbf{2}}{3 \times \mathbf{2}} = \frac{2}{6}$$

7.2 SUBTRACTING FRACTIONS WITH UNLIKE DENOMINATORS

Use the diagram to subtract the fractions:

$$\frac{5}{6} - \frac{2}{6} = \frac{3}{6}$$

Reduce $\frac{3}{6}$ to simplest form:

$$\frac{3}{6} = \frac{3 \div \mathbf{3}}{6 \div \mathbf{3}} = \frac{1}{2}$$

Mary used $\frac{1}{2}$ gallon of blue paint.

- -

RULE: *How to subtract two fractions with <u>unlike</u> denominators.*

---

1. **Change the fractions to fractions with like denominators.**

2. **Subtract the numerators.**

3. **The difference of the fractions is this fraction:**

   $$\frac{\text{Difference of the numerators}}{\text{Like denominator}}$$

4. **Simplify the answer if you can.**

EXAMPLE

Subtract: $\frac{5}{6} - \frac{1}{4} = ?$

1. The LCD for 4 and 6 is 12. Change both fractions to fractions with denominators of 12.

   $$\frac{5}{6} = \frac{5 \times \mathbf{2}}{6 \times \mathbf{2}} = \frac{10}{12} \qquad \frac{1}{4} = \frac{1 \times \mathbf{3}}{4 \times \mathbf{3}} = \frac{3}{12}$$

2. Subtract the numerators.

   $$10 - 3 = 7$$

3. The difference of $\frac{5}{6} - \frac{1}{4}$ is

   $$\frac{10 - \mathbf{3}}{12} = \frac{7}{12}$$

4. $\frac{7}{12}$ cannot be simplified.

The answer is $\frac{7}{12}$.

7. SUBTRACTING FRACTIONS

Exercises with Hints

Put a check mark before the exercises that show fractions with <u>unlike</u> denominators.
(Hint: Two denominators are <u>unlike</u> if they are different.)

1. ☐ $\frac{1}{2}$ − $\frac{2}{5}$

2. ☐ $\frac{7}{10}$ − $\frac{3}{10}$

3. ☐ $\frac{5}{7}$ − $\frac{7}{20}$

4. ☐ $\frac{7}{23}$ − $\frac{23}{27}$

5. ☐ $\frac{9}{10}$ − $\frac{10}{9}$

6. ☐ $\frac{5}{6}$ − $\frac{1}{3}$

Change the fractions to equivalent fractions with denominators of 12.
(Hint: What number do you multiply each denominator by to get 12?)

7. $\frac{1}{2}$ _____

8. $\frac{1}{6}$ _____

9. $\frac{3}{4}$ _____

Change the fractions to equivalent fractions with denominators of 20.
(Hint: What number do you multiply each denominator by to get 20?)

10. $\frac{3}{10}$ _____

11. $\frac{4}{5}$ _____

12. $\frac{1}{4}$ _____

Subtract the fractions.
(Hint: Use the steps in the Example section before the Exercises.)

13. $\frac{2}{3}$ − $\frac{1}{6}$ = _____

14. $\frac{7}{12}$ − $\frac{1}{4}$ = _____

15. $\frac{7}{15}$ − $\frac{2}{5}$ = _____

16. $\frac{17}{20}$ − $\frac{3}{5}$ = _____

17. $\frac{11}{25}$ − $\frac{2}{5}$ = _____

18. $\frac{4}{5}$ − $\frac{1}{2}$ = _____

19. $\frac{3}{7}$ − $\frac{1}{4}$ = _____

20. $\frac{14}{15}$ − $\frac{1}{4}$ = _____

21. $\frac{7}{8}$ − $\frac{1}{3}$ = _____

Solve.

22. By mistake, Arturo used $\frac{1}{2}$ cup of water in a recipe even though the recipe called for $\frac{7}{8}$ cup. How much less than the amount in the recipe did he use?

(Hint: Change $\frac{1}{2}$ to the equivalent fraction in eighths and subtract numerators.)

_____

128

7.2 SUBTRACTING FRACTIONS WITH UNLIKE DENOMINATORS

23. Barbara saves $\frac{1}{6}$ of her salary, while Michelle saves $\frac{1}{7}$ of her salary.

   a. Who saves more, Barbara or Michelle? _____

   b. What fraction more? _____

(Hint: You can answer Question a by using the method described in Lesson 1.4. But to answer Question b, you have to change both fractions to equivalent fractions with the same denominator and subtract numerators.)

Exercises on Your Own

Change the fractions to equivalent fractions with denominators of **30**.

1. $\frac{3}{15}$ _____

2. $\frac{5}{6}$ _____

3. $\frac{3}{5}$ _____

Change the fractions to equivalent fractions with denominators of **24**.

4. $\frac{7}{12}$ _____

5. $\frac{5}{6}$ _____

6. $\frac{1}{4}$ _____

Change the fractions to equivalent fractions with denominators of **28**.

7. $\frac{2}{7}$ _____

8. $\frac{1}{4}$ _____

9. $\frac{3}{14}$ _____

Subtract the fractions.

10. $\frac{4}{5} - \frac{1}{3} =$ _____

11. $\frac{7}{9} - \frac{1}{3} =$ _____

12. $\frac{13}{30} - \frac{1}{5} =$ _____

13. $\frac{7}{24} - \frac{1}{4} =$ _____

14. $\frac{27}{28} - \frac{3}{14} =$ _____

15. $\frac{6}{7} - \frac{3}{4} =$ _____

16. $\frac{11}{15} - \frac{1}{2} =$ _____

17. $\frac{7}{8} - \frac{1}{3} =$ _____

18. $\frac{14}{15} - \frac{1}{2} =$ _____

Solve.

19. Katrice read $\frac{2}{5}$ of the sales manual for her new job. George read $\frac{1}{3}$ of the manual.

   a. Who read more, Katrice or George? _____

   b. How much more? _____

129

7. SUBTRACTING FRACTIONS

20. It took Harold's computer $\frac{1}{30}$ of a second to complete the computation he wanted. It took Jane's computer $\frac{1}{15}$ of a second to complete the same computation.

   a. Which computer was faster? _____

   b. By how much? _____

21. Greg has $\frac{4}{5}$ pound of sugar. He used $\frac{1}{3}$ pound to make cookies. How much sugar does he have left?

_____

7.3 Subtracting Mixed Numbers with Unlike Denominators

When you subtract mixed numbers, you go through the same steps that you do when you add them. You first subtract the whole number parts, then you subtract the fraction parts, and finally you combine the two answers.

There are two kinds of mixed-number subtraction problems that you have to look out for, however. You will see them in Examples 1 and 2 below.

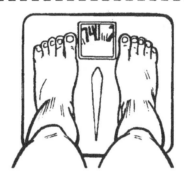

Bart weighed $78\frac{3}{4}$ pounds last week. Now he weighs $74\frac{1}{8}$ pounds. How many pounds did he lose?

To find the answer, subtract:

$$78\frac{3}{4} - 74\frac{1}{8} = \ ?$$

To subtract two mixed numbers, first write the mixed numbers under each other:

$$\begin{array}{r} 78\frac{3}{4} \\ -\ 74\frac{1}{8} \\ \hline ? \end{array}$$

You should subtract the fraction parts first, then the whole number parts second.

To subtract the fractions, change the fractions to equivalent fractions with <u>like</u> denominators.

Change $\frac{3}{4}$ to $\frac{6}{8}$. Then subtract the fractions first:

$$\begin{array}{r} 78\frac{3}{4} \\ -\ 74\frac{1}{8} \end{array} \longrightarrow \begin{array}{r} 78\frac{6}{8} \\ 74\frac{1}{8} \\ \hline \frac{5}{8} \end{array}$$

131

7. SUBTRACTING FRACTIONS

Next, subtract the whole numbers:

$$78\frac{3}{4} \longrightarrow 78\frac{6}{8}$$
$$- 74\frac{1}{8} \longrightarrow 74\frac{1}{8}$$
$$4\frac{5}{8}$$

The answer is $4\frac{5}{8}$. It cannot be simplified.

Bart lost $4\frac{5}{8}$ pounds.

- -

RULE: *How to subtract two mixed numbers:*

1. *Write the mixed numbers under each other.*

2. *Subtract the fractions.*

3. *Subtract the whole numbers.*

4. *Simplify the answer.*

EXAMPLE 1

Subtract: $7\frac{2}{9} - 3\frac{1}{3}$

1. Write the mixed numbers under each other.

$$7\frac{2}{9}$$
$$- 3\frac{1}{3}$$

2. Subtract the fractions. But look out! There's a problem with the fraction parts of the mixed numbers!

$$7\frac{2}{9} \longrightarrow 7\frac{2}{9}$$
$$- 3\frac{1}{3} \longrightarrow - 3\frac{3}{9}$$

Notice that we cannot subtract $\frac{3}{9}$ from $\frac{2}{9}$!

To subtract the fractions, rewrite the whole number 7 as $6\frac{9}{9}$.

Then add the $\frac{2}{9}$ to the $\frac{9}{9}$:

$$7\frac{2}{9} \longrightarrow (6 + \frac{9}{9}) + \frac{2}{9} \longrightarrow 6\frac{11}{9}$$
$$- 3\frac{3}{9} \longrightarrow - 3 + \frac{3}{9} \longrightarrow - 3\frac{3}{9}$$
$$\cdots \frac{8}{9}$$

Look carefully at this step until you are sure you understand it.

132

3. Subtract the whole numbers.

$$6\frac{11}{9}$$
$$-\ 3\frac{3}{9}$$
$$\overline{\quad\ 3\frac{8}{9}}$$

4. You don't need to simplify the difference, since the answer $3\frac{8}{9}$ is already in simplest form.

EXAMPLE 2

Subtract: $10 - 4\frac{4}{5} = ?$

This is an example of subtracting a mixed number from a whole number.

1. Write the numbers under each other.

$$10$$
$$-\ 4\frac{4}{5}$$
$$\overline{}$$

2. Subtract the fractions. To subtract $\frac{4}{5}$ we need to rewrite 10 as:

$$10 = 9 + \frac{5}{5} = 9\frac{5}{5}$$

$$10 \longrightarrow 9\frac{5}{5}$$
$$-\ 4\frac{4}{5} \longrightarrow -\ 4\frac{4}{5}$$
$$\overline{} \qquad \overline{\quad \cdots \frac{1}{5}}$$

3. Subtract the whole numbers.

$$9\frac{5}{5}$$
$$-\ 4\frac{4}{5}$$
$$\overline{\quad\ 5\frac{1}{5}}$$

4. You don't need to simplify the difference, since the answer $5\frac{1}{5}$ is already in simplest form.

7. SUBTRACTING FRACTIONS

Exercises with Hints

Put a check mark before the exercises that show subtraction of two mixed numbers.
(Hint: A mixed number consists of a whole number and a fraction.)

1. ☐ $5\frac{6}{7} - 1\frac{1}{3}$

2. ☐ $8 - 3\frac{3}{4}$

3. ☐ $17 - 9\frac{5}{8}$

4. ☐ $22\frac{1}{2} - 10\frac{2}{7}$

5. ☐ $8\frac{7}{8} - 4\frac{2}{5}$

6. ☐ $33\frac{7}{8} - \frac{7}{8}$

Put a check mark before the exercises that show mixed numbers that have fractional parts with <u>like</u> denominators.
*(Hint: Remember that denominators that are exactly the same are called **like** denominators.)*

7. ☐ $4\frac{5}{8} - 2\frac{1}{8}$

8. ☐ $17\frac{7}{8} - 10\frac{5}{6}$

9. ☐ $20\frac{4}{15} - 1\frac{1}{15}$

10. ☐ $100 - 3\frac{1}{2}$

The fractions in Exercises 11-12 are fractions with <u>like</u> denominators. Subtract the mixed numbers.
(Hint: Write the second mixed number below the first. Then follow the rules for subtracting like fractions.)

11. $14\frac{3}{5} - 12\frac{1}{5} =$ _____

12. $25\frac{7}{9} - 2\frac{4}{9} =$ _____

The fractions in Exercises 13-14 are fractions with <u>unlike</u> denominators. Subtract the mixed numbers.

13. $7\frac{3}{4} - 4\frac{1}{3} =$ _____

(Hint: First change the fractions to equivalent fractions with <u>like</u> denominators. Then subtract.)

14. $5\frac{3}{10} - 1\frac{2}{5} =$ _____

(Hint: Follow the steps in Example 1.)

15. $7 - 5\frac{2}{3} =$ _____

(Hint: Follow the steps in Example 2.)

Solve.

16. Lien filled her car up with $12\frac{3}{4}$ gallons of gas before her trip. After driving for 7 hours, she filled the car up again. This time the amount was $10\frac{7}{8}$ gallons. How much more did she put in the car the first time she filled up? *(Hint: Follow the steps in Example 1.)*

_____

7.3 SUBTRACTING MIXED NUMBERS WITH UNLIKE DENOMINATORS

Exercises on Your Own

Put a check mark before the exercises that show mixed numbers that have fractional parts with <u>like</u> denominators.

1. ☐ $6\frac{5}{7} - 2\frac{3}{7}$

2. ☐ $13\frac{8}{9} - 10\frac{1}{8}$

3. ☐ $100\frac{1}{100} - 10\frac{7}{100}$

4. ☐ $8\frac{5}{8} - 2\frac{8}{9}$

The fractions in Exercises 5-8 are fractions with <u>like</u> denominators. Subtract the mixed numbers.

5. $4\frac{5}{8} - 2\frac{1}{8} =$ _____

6. $8\frac{9}{10} - 2\frac{3}{10} =$ _____

7. $10\frac{4}{23} - 1\frac{1}{23} =$ _____

8. $18\frac{18}{19} - 17\frac{17}{19} =$ _____

9. $12\frac{13}{15} - 10\frac{11}{15} =$ _____

10. $6\frac{4}{7} - 6\frac{3}{7} =$ _____

The fractions in Exercises 11-14 are fractions with <u>unlike</u> denominators. Subtract the mixed numbers.

11. $10\frac{3}{10} - 2\frac{1}{5} =$ _____

12. $40\frac{1}{24} - 10\frac{5}{12} =$ _____

13. $8\frac{4}{9} - 2\frac{1}{6} =$ _____

14. $11\frac{11}{15} - 1\frac{1}{2} =$ _____

15. $8 - 5\frac{3}{10} =$ _____

16. $16\frac{3}{7} - 2\frac{2}{3} =$ _____

Solve.

17. Kathy took $13\frac{3}{4}$ hours researching and writing a report. She spent $1\frac{1}{2}$ hours revising and typing it with a word processor. How much longer did she it take to research and write the paper than to revise and type it?

_____

18. Connie spoke to the City Council for $2\frac{5}{6}$ hours, and then went to lunch for $\frac{3}{4}$ hours. How much more time did she spend speaking than eating?

_____

7.4 Review

Subtract these fractions with like denominators.

1. $\dfrac{3}{5} - \dfrac{1}{5} =$ _____

2. $\dfrac{4}{11} - \dfrac{2}{11} =$ _____

3. $\dfrac{13}{15} - \dfrac{2}{15} =$ _____

4. $\dfrac{7}{8} - \dfrac{7}{8} =$ _____

Subtract these fractions with unlike denominators.

5. $\dfrac{11}{12} - \dfrac{3}{4} =$ _____

6. $\dfrac{7}{9} - \dfrac{2}{3} =$ _____

7. $\dfrac{14}{15} - \dfrac{1}{6} =$ _____

8. $\dfrac{7}{10} - \dfrac{4}{15} =$ _____

Subtract these fractions.

9. $\dfrac{5}{8} - \dfrac{1}{4} =$ _____

10. $\dfrac{8}{9} - \dfrac{5}{12} =$ _____

11. $\dfrac{13}{15} - \dfrac{1}{5} =$ _____

12. $\dfrac{5}{8} - \dfrac{2}{5} =$ _____

13. $\dfrac{17}{18} - \dfrac{4}{9} =$ _____

14. $\dfrac{16}{23} - \dfrac{5}{23} =$ _____

Subtract these mixed numbers that have fractions with like denominators.

15. $4\dfrac{4}{5} - 1\dfrac{2}{5} =$ _____

16. $20\dfrac{11}{12} - 15\dfrac{7}{12} =$ _____

17. $5\dfrac{2}{3} - 1\dfrac{2}{3} =$ _____

18. $8\dfrac{6}{7} - 1\dfrac{3}{7} =$ _____

Subtract these mixed numbers that have fractions with unlike denominators.

19. $4\dfrac{3}{14} - 2\dfrac{1}{7} =$ _____

20. $7\dfrac{5}{18} - 2\dfrac{1}{2} =$ _____

21. $18\dfrac{3}{5} - 12\dfrac{2}{7} =$ _____

22. $40\dfrac{7}{9} - 30\dfrac{3}{4} =$ _____

Subtract these mixed numbers.

23. $9\dfrac{5}{8} - 1\dfrac{1}{4} =$ _____

24. $4\dfrac{3}{5} - 1\dfrac{1}{5} =$ _____

25. $33\dfrac{2}{9} - 30\dfrac{5}{9} =$ _____

26. $8\dfrac{1}{3} - 5\dfrac{4}{9} =$ _____

27. $4\dfrac{4}{5} - 2\dfrac{7}{8} =$ _____

7.4 REVIEW

Solve. Write all your answers as fractions or mixed numbers.

27. Ossie worked for $\frac{3}{4}$ of an hour and rested for $\frac{1}{6}$ of an hour. How much longer did he work than he rested?

_____

28. Leroy received $\frac{5}{6}$ of the votes for district leader. Jane received $\frac{1}{10}$ of the votes.

a. Who received more votes, Leroy or Jane? _____

b. How much more? _____

29. Felix drank $3\frac{3}{4}$ cups of juice in the morning and $1\frac{7}{8}$ cups in the evening. How many more cups did he drink in the morning?

_____

30. Juana saw two movies last Saturday. The mystery lasted $2\frac{1}{5}$ hours, and the comedy lasted $1\frac{7}{8}$ hours.

a. Which was longer, the mystery or the comedy? _____

b. How much longer? _____

31. The math part of the test to get a license in the carpenter's union was $2\frac{1}{2}$ pages long. The rest of the test was $3\frac{3}{4}$ pages long.

a. Which part was longer, the math test or the rest of the test?

_____

b. How much longer? _____

8. Multiplying Fractions

8.1 The Fractional Part of a Number

A common use for fractions is in a problem like this one: "What is $\frac{1}{3}$ of 24?" This is called **"finding a fractional part of a number."** The lesson will show you how to solve problems like this one.

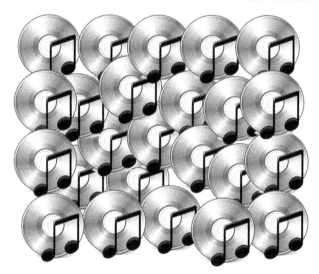

Juan bought 24 music disks.

Now he has only $\frac{1}{3}$ of the disks left.

How many does he have left?

To find $\frac{1}{3}$ of 24, divide the group of 24 into 3 equal groups:

Each group has 8 disks in it.

Juan has 8 disks left.

You can get the answer directly by dividing 24 by 3, the number of equal groups:

$24 \div 3 = 8$

8.1 THE FRACTIONAL PART OF A NUMBER

RULE: *How to find a fractional part of a whole number <u>when the numerator</u> <u>of the fraction is 1:</u>*

Divide the whole number by the denominator of the fraction.

EXAMPLE 1

Find $\frac{1}{5}$ of $35.

The whole number is 35 and the denominator of the fraction is 5.

The numerator of the fraction is 1, so you can divide.

Divide 35 by 5, the denominator of the fraction:
$$35 \div 5 = 7$$

$\frac{1}{5}$ of $35 is $7.

EXAMPLE 2

Find $\frac{1}{9}$ of 279 people.

The whole number is 279 and the denominator is 9.

The numerator of the fraction is 1, so you can divide.

Divide 279 by 9:

$$
\begin{array}{r}
31 \\
9\ \overline{)\ 279} \\
-27 \\
\hline
9 \\
-9 \\
\hline
0
\end{array}
$$

$\frac{1}{9}$ of 279 people is 31 people.

Exercises with Hints _____

What is the denominator of each fraction?
(Hint: Remember, the denominator is the bottom part of the fraction.)

1. $\frac{1}{7}$ _____

2. $\frac{1}{23}$ _____

3. $\frac{5}{8}$ _____

8. MULTIPLYING FRACTIONS

Circle the correct method for finding the answer for each exercise in 4-6.
(Hint: Check the rule in this lesson.)

4. $\frac{1}{7}$ of 49

   a. 49 + 7

   b. 7 + 49

   c. 49 + 7

5. $\frac{1}{12}$ of 348

   a. 12 × 348

   b. 348 ÷ 12

   c. 348 – 12

6. $\frac{1}{6}$ of 6

   a. 6 + 6

   b. 6 + 1

   c. 1 + 1

7. The rule of this lesson about finding a fractional part of a whole number applies to a special kind of fractions. Cross out any of the following fractions that are not fractions of this kind. *(Hint: Read the rule again.)*

$$\frac{1}{7} \qquad \frac{2}{11} \qquad \frac{3}{5} \qquad \frac{1}{8} \qquad \frac{1}{10}$$

Find the fractional part of each whole number.
(Hint: Use the same method as in the examples. Divide the whole number by the denominator of the fraction.)

8. $\frac{1}{2}$ of 24 = _____

9. $\frac{1}{3}$ of 18 = _____

10. $\frac{1}{12}$ of 36 = _____

11. $\frac{1}{5}$ of 50 = _____

12. $\frac{1}{10}$ of 40 = _____

13. $\frac{1}{6}$ of 30 = _____

14. $\frac{1}{2}$ of 20 = _____

15. $\frac{1}{3}$ of 30 = _____

16. $\frac{1}{5}$ of 45 = _____

17. $\frac{1}{7}$ of 343 = _____

Solve.

18. Aliza said that $\frac{1}{5}$ of the 400 pounds of paper can be recycled. How many pounds can be recycled? *(Hint: Follow the rule. Divide 400 by 5.)*

_____

19. David is a waiter in a restaurant where there are 45 tables. He is responsible for $\frac{1}{9}$ of the tables. How many tables is he responsible for? *(Hint: Follow the rule. Divide the whole number by the denominator of the fraction.)*

_____

8.1 THE FRACTIONAL PART OF A NUMBER

Exercises on Your Own

Select the correct method to find the answer for each exercise in 4-6.

1. $\frac{1}{8}$ of 32 = ?

   a. 32 ÷ 8

   b. 32 × 8

   c. 32 – 8

2. $\frac{1}{4}$ of 24 = ?

   a. 4 ÷ 24

   b. 24 ÷ 4

   c. 24 – 4

3. $\frac{1}{16}$ of 64 = ?

   a. 16 + 64

   b. 64 – 16

   c. 64 ÷ 16

4. Complete this statement of the rule of this lesson:

   When the numerator of the fraction is _____ , divide the whole number by the denominator of the fraction.

Find the fractional part of each whole number.

5. $\frac{1}{3}$ of 15 = _____

6. $\frac{1}{4}$ of 16 = _____

7. $\frac{1}{10}$ of 50 = _____

8. $\frac{1}{4}$ of 20 = _____

9. $\frac{1}{6}$ of 30 = _____

10. $\frac{1}{9}$ of 45 = _____

Solve.

11. Curt bought 75 baseball cards. He put $\frac{1}{5}$ of these into his album. How many did he put into his album?

    _____

12. Nancy made 56 phone calls on Monday. $\frac{1}{8}$ of the calls were long distance calls. How many calls were long distance?

    _____

13. Erika read 40 pages on tax law yesterday. Only $\frac{1}{10}$ of the pages were useful to her. How many pages were useful?

    _____

14. $\frac{1}{5}$ of the 4500 people at a basketball game were students. How many people were students?

    _____

8.2 Multiplying a Whole Number by a Fraction

Suppose the fraction you multiply by does not have 1 as a numerator. How do you multiply? This lesson will show you how.

Reggie carried 5 envelopes to the post office.

Each envelope weighed $\frac{3}{4}$ pound.

How much did the envelopes weigh altogether?

There are two ways to find the answer.

One way is to add $\frac{3}{4}$ five times:

$$\frac{3}{4} + \frac{3}{4} + \frac{3}{4} + \frac{3}{4} + \frac{3}{4} = \frac{15}{4}$$

The envelopes are $\frac{15}{4}$ pounds altogether.

Simplified, that equals $3\frac{3}{4}$ pounds.

A better way to solve the problem is to multiply:

$$5 \times \frac{3}{4} = ?$$

The multiplication states 5 times $\frac{3}{4}$, or 5 × 3-fourths, or 15-fourths:

$$5 \times \frac{3}{4} = \frac{15}{4}$$

Simplify. Change $\frac{15}{4}$ to $3\frac{3}{4}$.

RULE: How to Multiply a Whole Number by Any Fraction:

1. Multiply the whole number by the <u>numerator</u> of the fraction.
2. Form a new fraction with the product and the denominator of the old fraction.
3. If necessary, change the fraction to a mixed number (simplify the fraction).

EXAMPLE 1

Multiply: $9 \times \dfrac{4}{5} = ?$

1. Multiply by the numerator: $9 \times 4 = 36$

2. Form a new fraction with the product and the denominator: $\dfrac{36}{5}$

3. Change to a mixed number: $\dfrac{36}{5} = 7\dfrac{1}{5}$

EXAMPLE 2

Multiply: $4 \times \dfrac{7}{100} = ?$

1. Multiply by the numerator: $4 \times 7 = 28$

2. Form a new fraction with the product and the denominator: $\dfrac{28}{100}$

3. Simplify the fraction:

$$\dfrac{28}{100} = \dfrac{28 \div 4}{100 \div 4} = \dfrac{7}{25}$$

EXAMPLE 3

Multiply: $\dfrac{3}{50} \times 15 = ?$

This example shows a fraction times a whole number.

This is the opposite order of the examples you have seen so far.

You can multiply two numbers in any order, so you don't have to worry that the whole number comes second in this example.

Just follow the steps of the rule.

1. Multiply the whole number by the numerator: $15 \times 3 = 45$

2. Put the answer over the denominator: $\dfrac{45}{50}$

3. Simplify: $\dfrac{45}{50} = \dfrac{9}{10}$

8. MULTIPLYING FRACTIONS

Exercises with Hints

Show how to add to find the answer.
(Hint: For example, $3 \times \frac{1}{3}$ means add $\frac{1}{3}$ three times.)

1. $3 \times \frac{1}{3}$ = **?** Add _____ times

2. $6 \times \frac{1}{2}$ = **?** Add _____ times

3. $4 \times \frac{1}{4}$ = **?** Add _____ times

Which numbers do you multiply to find the product? (Hint: Check the first step in the RULE section.)

4. $35 \times \frac{7}{8}$ = **?**

Multiply _____ and _____

5. $78 \times \frac{7}{11}$ = **?**

Multiply _____ and _____

6. $9 \times \frac{89}{100}$ = **?**

Multiply _____ and _____

Which numbers do you multiply to find the products?
(Hint: Check the rule for Step 1.)

7. $\frac{5}{8} \times 235$ = **?**

Multiply _____ and _____

8. $\frac{12}{13} \times 125$ = **?**

Multiply _____ and _____

9. $\frac{3}{35} \times 8$ = **?**

Multiply _____ and _____

Multiply.
(Hint: Follow the rule: Multiply numerators. Place answers over the denominator. Simplify.)

10. $5 \times \frac{2}{3}$ = _____

11. $6 \times \frac{3}{4}$ = _____

12. $8 \times \frac{5}{6}$ = _____

Multiply.
(Hint: Follow Example 3 above.)

13. $\frac{1}{5} \times 31$ = _____

14. $\frac{2}{7} \times 63$ = _____

15. $\frac{4}{5} \times 11$ = _____

Solve.

16. Joanna is a sales rep for a large toy manufacturer. She has 23 phone calls to make to customers. She estimates that each call will take $\frac{1}{10}$ of an hour. How long will all 23 phone calls take?
(Hint: Multiply whole number times numerator . . . Divide . . . Write as a mixed number.)

_____

17. Jan solved $\frac{1}{3}$ of 135 problems. How many problems did she solve?
(Hint: Follow Example 3.)

_____

144

8.2 MULTIPLYING A WHOLE NUMBER BY A FRACTION

18. Betty Ann is on a special diet. She must have $\frac{1}{4}$ pound of fish every day. How many pounds of fish will she eat in 2 weeks?

(Hint: How many days in a week? In two weeks?)

_____

Exercises on Your Own

Show how to add to find the answer.

1. $5 \times \frac{1}{4} = ?$ _____

2. $4 \times \frac{2}{3} = ?$ _____

3. $6 \times \frac{4}{5} = ?$ _____

Multiply.

4. $6 \times \frac{4}{5} =$ _____

5. $\frac{3}{80} \times 12 =$ _____

6. $12 \times \frac{7}{8} =$ _____

7. $4 \times \frac{8}{9} =$ _____

8. $\frac{7}{10} \times 20 =$ _____

9. $3 \times \frac{1}{9} =$ _____

10. $15 \times \frac{2}{3} =$ _____

11. $8 \times \frac{3}{5} =$ _____

12. $\frac{4}{11} \times 27 =$ _____

Solve.

13. Vicki has 11 boxes of computer disks. Each box weighs $\frac{3}{4}$ pound. How much do all the boxes weigh?

_____

14. Jack exercised for 68 minutes. One fourth of the time he did push-ups? For how many minutes did he do push-ups?

_____

15. Burt ran 16 laps around the track. Each lap is $\frac{1}{3}$ of a mile. How far did Burt run?

_____

16. Sandy has 8 chapters to read in her sales training manual. She estimates that each chapter will take $\frac{2}{5}$ hour. About how long will the 8 chapters take?

_____

17. Eight-ninths of the graduating class went to a basketball game. There are 216 people in the graduating class. How many people went to the basketball game?

_____

8.3 Multiplying Two Fractions

In this lesson, you will learn how to multiply two fractions. As you will see, multiplying fractions is actually easier than adding them.

Ozzie has to read half of a training manual in the next two weeks.

He decides to read $\frac{1}{3}$ of the half this week.

What fraction of the whole manual will he read this week?

To solve the problem, find $\frac{1}{3}$ of $\frac{1}{2}$.

To find $\frac{1}{3}$ of $\frac{1}{2}$, study the diagrams:

1.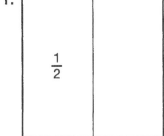
2.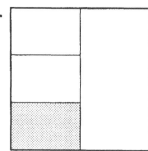
3.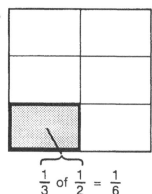

$\frac{1}{3}$ of $\frac{1}{2}$ = $\frac{1}{6}$

Ozzie will read $\frac{1}{6}$ of the book this week.

RULE 1: What does "of" mean?

> **When we use "of" with fractions, it means <u>multiply</u>:**
>
> $\frac{1}{3}$ <u>of</u> $\frac{1}{2}$ means $\frac{1}{3} \times \frac{1}{2}$

8.3 MULTIPLYING TWO FRACTIONS

RULE 2: *How to multiply two fractions:*

> 1. *Multiply the two numerators.*
>
> 2. *Multiply the two denominators.*
>
> 3. *Form a fraction from the results of 1 and 2:*
>
> $$\frac{\text{Product of numerators}}{\text{Product of denominators}}$$
>
> 4. *Simplify the fraction.*

EXAMPLE 1

Find $\frac{2}{5}$ of $\frac{1}{4}$.

Remember **RULE 1**, above: $\frac{2}{5}$ *of* $\frac{1}{4}$ means $\frac{2}{5} \times \frac{1}{4}$.

Follow **RULE 2:**

   1. Multiply numerators: $2 \times 1 = 2$

   2. Multiply denominators: $5 \times 4 = 20$

   3. Make a new fraction from the products: $\frac{2}{20}$

   4. Simplify: $\frac{2}{20} = \frac{1}{10}$

The method you just learned also works when you multiply a whole number times a fraction. Just change the whole number into a fraction with the denominator 1. For example, you would change a whole number like 5 into $\frac{5}{1}$. Then follow **RULE 2.**

EXAMPLE 2

Find $\frac{7}{10}$ of 20.

$\frac{7}{10}$ of 20 means $\frac{7}{10} \times \frac{20}{1}$. (You change the whole number into a fraction.)

   1. Multiply the numerators of the fractions: $7 \times 20 = 140$

   2. Multiply denominators: $10 \times 1 = 10$

   3. Make a new fraction from the products: $\frac{140}{10}$

   4. Simplify: $\frac{140}{10} = 14$

8. MULTIPLYING FRACTIONS

Exercises with Hints

Rewrite each of the following as a multiplication problem.
(Hint: Remember RULE 1: of means "multiply.")

1. $\frac{3}{5}$ of $\frac{7}{8}$ _____

2. $\frac{1}{7}$ of $\frac{9}{10}$ _____

3. $\frac{8}{13}$ of $\frac{1}{5}$ _____

Rewrite each as a multiplication problem, changing the whole number into a fraction.
(Hint: Rewrite the whole number as a fraction with the denominator 1.)

4. $\frac{1}{3} \times 15$ _____

5. $\frac{2}{3}$ of 21 _____

6. $15 \times \frac{3}{5}$ _____

What is the numerator of the product?
(Hint: See Step 1 of RULE 2, above.)

7. $\frac{5}{8} \times \frac{2}{3}$ = **?** The numerator

of the product is: _____

8. $\frac{9}{20} \times \frac{1}{7}$ = **?** The numerator

of the product is: _____

9. $\frac{3}{8} \times \frac{7}{8}$ = **?** The numerator

of the product is: _____

What is the denominator of the product?
(Hint: See Step 2 of RULE 2, above.)

10. $\frac{3}{7} \times \frac{1}{5}$ = **?** The denominator

of the product is: _____

11. $\frac{6}{11} \times \frac{2}{7}$ = **?** The denominator

of the product is: _____

12. $\frac{1}{2} \times \frac{1}{5}$ = **?** The denominator

of the product is: _____

Multiply.
(Hint: Follow the 4 steps of RULE 2. Remember to simplify if you can.)

13. $\frac{1}{4}$ of $\frac{3}{5}$ = _____

14. $\frac{3}{7}$ of $\frac{1}{2}$ = _____

15. $\frac{1}{3}$ of $\frac{6}{7}$ = _____

16. $\frac{3}{7}$ of 14 = _____

Solve.

17. Pedro wants to plant vegetables on $\frac{3}{4}$ of his backyard. $\frac{1}{3}$ of the area for vegetables will be for tomatoes. What fraction of the yard will have tomatoes?
(Hint: Follow RULES 1 and 2.)

_____

148

8.3 MULTIPLYING TWO FRACTIONS

Exercises on Your Own

Multiply.

1. $\frac{2}{3}$ of $\frac{1}{7}$ = _____

2. $\frac{4}{7}$ of $\frac{1}{2}$ = _____

3. $\frac{1}{8}$ of $\frac{9}{10}$ = _____

4. $\frac{1}{6} \times \frac{7}{8}$ = _____

5. $\frac{2}{5} \times \frac{5}{6}$ = _____

6. $\frac{12}{25} \times \frac{4}{5}$ = _____

7. $\frac{2}{5} \times \frac{1}{3}$ = _____

8. $\frac{3}{10} \times \frac{1}{4}$ = _____

9. $\frac{3}{20} \times \frac{1}{2}$ = _____

Solve.

10. Willie had $\frac{1}{2}$ of the money he earned last week. He deposited $\frac{1}{5}$ of it. What fraction of all the money did he deposit?

_____

11. There are 35 players on the team. One-fifth of the players wore new sneakers. How many wore new sneakers?

_____

12. Mabel learned a fourth of the piano piece. She practiced $\frac{1}{3}$ of this part over and over. What fraction of the entire piece did she practice?

_____

13. Lawana was handing out pads of paper. She gave $\frac{1}{3}$ of the pads to Elvis. Elvis gave $\frac{1}{3}$ of his pads to Motoni. What fraction of the total number of pads did Motoni get?

_____

149

8.4 Writing Mixed Numbers as Fractions Greater Than 1

In the following lessons, you will learn how to multiply mixed numbers. First, however, you need to know how to change a mixed number into a fraction greater than 1. Doing this is the first step in multiplying mixed numbers.

Manny runs around a track at school that is $\frac{1}{4}$ mile long.

On Tuesday he ran $2\frac{3}{4}$ miles.

Write the mixed number $2\frac{3}{4}$ as a fraction greater than 1.

REMEMBER:

A **fraction greater than 1** is a fraction with the numerator greater than the denominator.

To change $2\frac{3}{4}$ to a fraction greater than 1, change 2 to fourths and then add $\frac{3}{4}$:

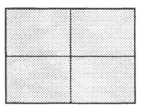 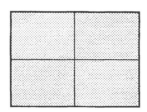 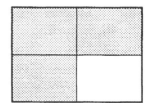

$$2\frac{3}{4} = 2 + \frac{3}{4} = \frac{8}{4} + \frac{3}{4} = \frac{11}{4}$$

The fraction $2\frac{3}{4}$ is equivalent to $\frac{11}{4}$.

What follows on the next page is a short cut to writing fractions greater than 1. Learn it!

8.4 WRITING MIXED NUMBERS AS FRACTIONS GREATER THAN 1

RULE: *How to write a mixed number as a fraction greater than 1:*

> 1. **Multiply the whole number part by the denominator.**
>
>   (For $2\frac{3}{4}$, $2 \times 4 = 8$)
>
> 2. **Add the numerator to the answer of Step 1.**
>
>   (For $2\frac{3}{4}$, $8 + 3 = 11$)
>
> 3. **Form the fraction:**
>
> $$\frac{\text{Answer from Step 2}}{\text{Denominator}}$$
>
>   (For $2\frac{3}{4} = \frac{11}{4}$)

EXAMPLE

Write $6\frac{2}{3}$ as a fraction greater than 1.

1. **Multiply** the whole number part by the denominator.

   $6 \times 3 = 18$

2. **Add** the numerator to the answer of Step 1.

   $18 + 2 = 20$

3. Form the fraction:

   $$\frac{20}{3}$$

So $6\frac{2}{3} = \frac{20}{3}$.

Exercises with Hints

Put a check mark after each mixed number. *(Hint: Remember, a mixed number has two parts.)*

1. $5\frac{1}{2}$ _____

2. $\frac{56}{23}$ _____

3. $\frac{9}{10}$ _____

4. $1\frac{1}{10}$ _____

5. $5\frac{1}{5}$ _____

6. $\frac{9}{4}$ _____

8. MULTIPLYING FRACTIONS

Put a check mark before each fraction greater than 1.

(Hint: The numerator is greater than the denominator in a fraction greater than 1.)

7. ☐ $\dfrac{1}{7}$

8. ☐ $\dfrac{3}{7}$

9. ☐ $\dfrac{7}{3}$

10. ☐ $\dfrac{5}{1}$

11. ☐ $\dfrac{10}{10}$

12. ☐ $\dfrac{18}{17}$

Write the whole number part of each mixed number.

13. $4\dfrac{5}{8}$ _____

14. $17\dfrac{3}{26}$ _____

15. $30\dfrac{1}{20}$ _____

16. $525\dfrac{7}{8}$ _____

17. $1\dfrac{9}{10}$ _____

Write the fraction part of each mixed number.

18. $9\dfrac{2}{3}$ _____

19. $12\dfrac{3}{4}$ _____

20. $9\dfrac{2}{7}$ _____

21. $1\dfrac{1}{9}$ _____

22. $875\dfrac{4}{5}$ _____

Write these mixed fractions as fractions greater than 1.

(Hint: Use the three steps in the Rule and the Examples, above.)

23. $1\dfrac{1}{5}$ = _____

24. $9\dfrac{2}{3}$ = _____

25. $4\dfrac{3}{5}$ = _____

26. $2\dfrac{7}{10}$ = _____

Write the mixed numbers in these statements as fractions greater than 1.

27. Alicia poured $3\dfrac{1}{3}$ cups of water into her fish tank.

_____

28. Randall takes a train to work each morning. The trip takes $1\dfrac{1}{4}$ hours.

_____

152

8.4 WRITING MIXED NUMBERS AS FRACTIONS GREATER THAN 1

Exercises on Your Own

Put a check mark before each mixed number.

1. ☐ $4\frac{4}{5}$

2. ☐ $3\frac{2}{9}$

3. ☐ $\frac{7}{6}$

4. ☐ $\frac{1}{2}$

5. ☐ $1\frac{6}{7}$

Put a check mark before each fraction greater than 1.

6. ☐ $\frac{5}{8}$

7. ☐ $\frac{4}{4}$

8. ☐ $\frac{11}{5}$

9. ☐ $\frac{6}{2}$

10. ☐ $\frac{9}{10}$

Write the following as fractions greater than 1.

11. $5\frac{1}{6}$ = _____

12. $1\frac{8}{9}$ = _____

13. $10\frac{5}{8}$ = _____

14. $7\frac{3}{5}$ = _____

15. $2\frac{3}{20}$ = _____

16. $15\frac{2}{7}$ = _____

17. $50\frac{2}{3}$ = _____

18. $8\frac{2}{11}$ = _____

19. $100\frac{1}{2}$ = _____

20. $3\frac{3}{4}$ = _____

Write the mixed numbers in these statements as fractions greater than 1.

21. Otto worked $12\frac{3}{10}$ hours last Saturday.

_____

22. Eartha listened to music for $1\frac{3}{5}$ hours.

_____

153

8.5 Multiplying by a Mixed Number

Now you are ready to learn how to multiply mixed numbers. As you will see, all you have to do is change the numbers into fractions greater than 1 and then multiply the fractions in the usual way.

Nissim carried $6\frac{1}{2}$ bags of flour into the kitchen.

A full bag weighs $2\frac{1}{4}$ pounds.

How many pounds of flour did he carry?

- To find the answer, multiply:
$$6\frac{1}{2} \times 2\frac{1}{4}$$
Both numbers are mixed numbers.

- Write each mixed number as a fraction greater than 1:
$$\frac{13}{2} \times \frac{9}{4}$$

- Follow the three steps for multiplying two fractions (See *Lesson 8.3*):
$$\frac{13}{2} \times \frac{9}{4} = \frac{13 \times 9}{2 \times 4} = \frac{117}{8}$$

- Change $\frac{117}{8}$ to a mixed number:
$$\frac{117}{8} = 14\frac{5}{8}$$

Nissim carried $14\frac{5}{8}$ pounds of flour.

8.5 MULTIPLYING BY A MIXED NUMBER

RULE: *How to multiply two mixed numbers:*

> 1. *Change the mixed numbers to fractions greater than 1.*
>
> 2. *Multiply the two fractions. (Use the steps of* Lesson 8.3.*)*
>
> 3. *Change the resulting fraction greater than 1 to a mixed number. (See* Lesson 3.3 *if you want a review of how to do this.)*

EXAMPLE 1

Multiply: $3\frac{1}{4} \times 2\frac{1}{2}$

1. Change the mixed numbers to fractions greater than 1.

$$\frac{13}{4} \times \frac{5}{2}$$

2. Multiply the two fractions.

$$\frac{13}{4} \times \frac{5}{2} = \frac{65}{8}$$

3. Change the resulting fraction greater than 1 to a mixed number.

$$\frac{65}{8} = 8\frac{1}{8}$$

EXAMPLE 2

Multiply: $\frac{1}{2} \times 2\frac{2}{3}$ (fraction $\times$ mixed number)

1. Change the mixed number to a fraction greater than 1.

$$\frac{1}{2} \times \frac{8}{3}$$

2. Multiply the two fractions.

$$\frac{1}{2} \times \frac{8}{3} = \frac{8}{6}$$

3. Change the resulting fraction greater than 1 to a mixed number.

$$\frac{8}{6} = 1\frac{2}{6} = 1\frac{1}{3}$$

8. MULTIPLYING FRACTIONS

Exercises with Hints

Put a check mark before the examples where two mixed numbers are being multiplied.
(Hint: Remember, a mixed number has two parts.)

1. ☐ $4\frac{2}{7} \times \frac{7}{8}$

2. ☐ $7\frac{1}{2} \times 1\frac{3}{4}$

3. ☐ $\frac{44}{3} \times \frac{7}{3}$

4. ☐ $\frac{5}{6} \times \frac{3}{11}$

5. ☐ $3\frac{1}{9} \times 76\frac{5}{6}$

6. ☐ $10\frac{2}{11} \times \frac{8}{7}$

Put a check mark before the examples where two <u>fractions</u> greater than 1 are being multiplied.
(Hint: The numerator of a fraction greater than 1 is greater than the denominator.)

7. ☐ $\frac{4}{3} \times \frac{7}{6}$

8. ☐ $1\frac{2}{7} \times \frac{8}{7}$

9. ☐ $4\frac{2}{7} \times \frac{6}{7}$

10. ☐ $\frac{9}{4} \times \frac{12}{11}$

11. ☐ $4\frac{2}{5} \times \frac{9}{5}$

12. ☐ $\frac{3}{11} \times \frac{9}{13}$

Multiply these fractions.
(Hint: Use the steps for multiplying two fractions described in Lesson 8.4.*)*

13. $\frac{2}{3} \times \frac{5}{6} =$ _____

14. $\frac{10}{11} \times \frac{1}{2} =$ _____

15. $\frac{3}{4} \times \frac{5}{6} =$ _____

Multiply (fraction greater than 1 $\times$ mixed number). *(Hint: Use the steps outlined in the Rule and Examples above.)*

16. $\frac{8}{7} \times 1\frac{1}{5} =$ _____

17. $\frac{3}{2} \times 2\frac{2}{5} =$ _____

18. $2\frac{2}{5} \times \frac{4}{3} =$ _____

Multiply (mixed number $\times$ mixed number). *(Hint: Use the steps outlined in the Rule and Examples above.)*

19. $4\frac{1}{3} \times 1\frac{1}{4} =$ _____

20. $2\frac{3}{10} \times 1\frac{1}{2} =$ _____

21. $1\frac{1}{9} \times 3\frac{1}{2} =$ _____

Solve.

22. Larry is on a weight reduction program. He plans to lose $3\frac{1}{2}$ pounds each month. How many pounds will he lose in $4\frac{1}{2}$ months? *(Hint: Use the steps outlined in the rule.)*

_____

156

Exercises on Your Own

Multiply.

1. $\dfrac{4}{7} \times \dfrac{3}{10} =$ _____

2. $\dfrac{5}{13} \times \dfrac{1}{5} =$ _____

3. $4\dfrac{1}{4} \times 1\dfrac{1}{5} =$ _____

4. $\dfrac{7}{8} \times \dfrac{1}{3} =$ _____

5. $\dfrac{11}{5} \times 2\dfrac{1}{3} =$ _____

6. $\dfrac{4}{3} \times \dfrac{7}{2} =$ _____

7. $1\dfrac{1}{2} \times 1\dfrac{1}{25} =$ _____

8. $2\dfrac{5}{6} \times 2\dfrac{1}{2} =$ _____

9. $\dfrac{3}{11} \times \dfrac{1}{5} =$ _____

Solve.

10. Dave has a special route for cycling. It is $5\dfrac{1}{5}$ miles long. On Tuesday of last week he made $3\dfrac{1}{2}$ trips around this bike route. How far did he go?

_____

11. Lisa runs laps around a course that is $1\dfrac{1}{5}$ mile long. How far does she go when she runs $8\dfrac{1}{2}$ laps?

_____

12. A can of house paint contains $1\dfrac{1}{2}$ gallons of paint. Paul used $4\dfrac{2}{3}$ cans. How much paint did he use?

_____

13. Velma spends $1\dfrac{1}{2}$ hours a day reading legal papers. How many hours does she do this after $6\dfrac{3}{4}$ days?

_____

8.6 Simplifying Before Multiplying

When you multiply mixed numbers, you first change the mixed numbers into fractions with numerators greater than 1. This can give you fractions with very large numerators that are difficult to multiply.

There is a shortcut that will help you—simplifying **before** you multiply. This lesson will show you how.

Melissa said she needs $7\frac{1}{2}$ times as much clay today as she used yesterday.

She used $2\frac{2}{3}$ pounds yesterday.

How much clay does she need today?

To find the answer, multiply:

$$7\frac{1}{2} \times 2\frac{2}{3} = ?$$

Start with the first two steps of Chapter 8, *Lesson 5.*

1. Change the mixed numbers to fractions greater than 1.

$$7\frac{1}{2} = \frac{15}{2}$$

$$2\frac{2}{3} = \frac{8}{3}$$

2. Multiply the two fractions.

$$\frac{15}{2} \times \frac{8}{3} = \frac{15 \times 8}{2 \times 3} = ?$$

But before you multiply, simplify the two fractions:

15 and 3 have a common factor—3.

Divide 15 and 3 by the common factor 3.

Do it like this:

$$\frac{15}{2} \times \frac{8}{3} = \frac{\overset{5}{\cancel{15}} \times 8}{2 \times \cancel{3}_{1}} = ?$$

8 and 2 have the same factor—2.

Divide 8 and 2 by the common factor 2.

Do it like this:

$$\frac{15}{2} \times \frac{8}{3} = \frac{\overset{5}{\cancel{15}} \times \overset{4}{\cancel{8}}}{\underset{1}{\cancel{2}} \times \underset{1}{\cancel{3}}} = ?$$

(This process of simplifying is sometimes called **canceling**.)

3. Now multiply:

$$\frac{\overset{5}{\cancel{15}} \times \overset{4}{\cancel{8}}}{\underset{1}{\cancel{2}} \times \underset{1}{\cancel{3}}} = \frac{20}{1}$$

4. Change the resulting fraction greater than 1 to a mixed number.

$$\frac{20}{1} = 20$$

When you simplify fractions before multiplying, you make multiplying easier.

You can divide by a common factor only if it is a factor of _both_ a numerator and a denominator of the two fractions.

- -

RULE: *How to simplify (cancel) before multiplying:*

> **1.** **Look for any common factors of either one of the numerators and either one of the denominators. If you can, make sure they are the greatest common factors.**
>
> **2.** **Divide the numerators and denominators by the common factors.**

EXAMPLE 1

$$\frac{7}{15} \times \frac{25}{49} = ?$$

Numerator 7 and denominator 49 have the same factor—7.

Divide both 7 and 49 by the common factor 7.

$$\frac{\overset{1}{\cancel{7}}}{15} \times \frac{25}{\underset{7}{\cancel{49}}} = ?$$

159

8. MULTIPLYING FRACTIONS

Denominator 15 and numerator 25 have the same factor—5.

Divide 15 and 25 by the common factor 5.

$$\overset{1}{\underset{3}{\cancel{\frac{7}{15}}}} \times \overset{5}{\underset{7}{\cancel{\frac{25}{49}}}} = \ ?$$

Multiply to get the answer:

$$\frac{1}{3} \times \frac{5}{7} = \frac{5}{21}$$

EXAMPLE 2

$$4\frac{7}{8} \times \frac{12}{27} = \ ?$$

Change the mixed number to a fraction greater than 1: $\frac{39}{8} \times \frac{12}{27} = \ ?$

Numerator 39 and denominator 27 have the same factor—3.

Divide 39 and 27 by the common factor 3.

$$\overset{13}{\cancel{\frac{39}{8}}} \times \underset{9}{\cancel{\frac{12}{27}}} = \ ?$$

Denominator 8 and numerator 12 have the same factors: 2 and 4.

But 4 is the greatest common factor (GCF).

Divide 8 and 12 by the GCF 4.

$$\overset{13}{\underset{2}{\cancel{\frac{39}{8}}}} \times \overset{3}{\underset{9}{\cancel{\frac{12}{27}}}} = \ ?$$

3 and 9 have the same factor—3.

Divide 3 and 9 by 3.

$$\overset{13}{\underset{2}{\cancel{\frac{39}{8}}}} \times \overset{1}{\underset{3}{\cancel{\frac{12}{27}}}} = \frac{13}{6}$$

Multiply to get the answer:

$$\frac{39}{8} \times \frac{12}{27} = \frac{13}{6} = 2\frac{1}{6}$$

We canceled three times to simplify before multiplying.

160

8.6 SIMPLIFYING BEFORE MULTIPLYING

Exercises with Hints

List all the common factors of each pair of numbers. *(Hint: Don't forget that 1 divides all numbers.)*

1. 14 and 22 _____

2. 30 and 45 _____

3. 8 and 28 _____

4. 17 and 18 _____

What is the GCF of these numbers? *(Hint: Remember, the GCF is the greatest number that divides both numbers.)*

5. 12 and 36 _____

6. 25 and 30 _____

7. 18 and 72 _____

8. 20 and 60 _____

Use canceling to reduce each fraction to lowest terms.
(Hint: Divide the numerator and denominator by the GCF.)

9. $\dfrac{15}{25}$ _____

10. $\dfrac{27}{36}$ _____

11. $\dfrac{33}{99}$ _____

12. $\dfrac{40}{80}$ _____

Simplify by canceling, then multiply. *(Hint: Divide either numerator and denominator by their GCF. Remember to change mixed numbers to fractions greater than 1 first.)*

13. $\dfrac{4}{7} \times \dfrac{28}{36} =$ _____

14. $4\dfrac{2}{5} \times \dfrac{30}{55} =$ _____

15. $6\dfrac{3}{10} \times 7\dfrac{2}{9} =$ _____

Solve.

16. Bernice wants to make each shelf of her bookcase $4\dfrac{2}{3}$ feet long. If Bernice builds 6 shelves, how many feet of shelving does she need? *(Hint: Write the mixed number as a fraction greater than 1. Then use canceling to simplify your work.)*

_____

8. MULTIPLYING FRACTIONS

Exercises on Your Own

Use canceling to reduce to lowest terms.

1. $\dfrac{28}{63}$ _____

2. $\dfrac{15}{45}$ _____

3. $\dfrac{42}{76}$ _____

4. $\dfrac{50}{75}$ _____

Simplify by canceling, then multiply.

5. $\dfrac{3}{7} \times \dfrac{21}{25} =$ _____

6. $\dfrac{7}{8} \times \dfrac{32}{42} =$ _____

7. $\dfrac{11}{12} \times 5\dfrac{1}{3} =$ _____

8. $13\dfrac{1}{3} \times 6\dfrac{3}{5} =$ _____

9. $6\dfrac{1}{8} \times 9\dfrac{1}{7} =$ _____

10. $\dfrac{4}{15} \times \dfrac{40}{50} =$ _____

Solve.

11. To paint her room, Marion needs $4\dfrac{1}{3}$ times as much paint as she has now. She has $\dfrac{3}{4}$ quart of paint now. How much paint does she need to paint her room?

_____

8.7 Review

Find the fractional part of each whole number.

1. $\frac{1}{2}$ of 24 = _____

2. $\frac{1}{3}$ of 24 = _____

3. $\frac{1}{5}$ of 75 = _____

4. $\frac{1}{4}$ of 36 = _____

5. $\frac{1}{10}$ of 400 = _____

Multiply. Simplify the answers.

6. $8 \times \frac{3}{5}$ = _____

7. $\frac{3}{10} \times 60$ = _____

8. $\frac{4}{7} \times 25$ = _____

9. $20 \times \frac{2}{3}$ = _____

10. $\frac{5}{6} \times 42$ = _____

Multiply. Simplify the answers.

11. $\frac{4}{7} \times \frac{1}{2}$ = _____

12. $\frac{3}{4} \times \frac{8}{9}$ = _____

13. $\frac{2}{5} \times \frac{5}{8}$ = _____

14. $\frac{6}{15} \times \frac{2}{3}$ = _____

15. $\frac{3}{8} \times \frac{9}{10}$ = _____

Which of these are mixed numbers?

16. $5\frac{1}{7}$ ___ yes ___ no

17. $\frac{12}{5}$ ___ yes ___ no

18. $\frac{9}{10}$ ___ yes ___ no

19. $10\frac{3}{13}$ ___ yes ___ no

20. 17 ___ yes ___ no

Which of these are fractions greater than 1?

21. $\frac{4}{9}$ ___ yes ___ no

22. $\frac{5}{3}$ ___ yes ___ no

23. $\frac{11}{5}$ ___ yes ___ no

24. $2\frac{1}{6}$ ___ yes ___ no

25. $\frac{1}{20}$ ___ yes ___ no

Write these as fractions greater than 1.

26. $4\frac{1}{5}$ _____

27. $1\frac{1}{7}$ _____

28. $9\frac{2}{3}$ _____

29. $5\frac{5}{6}$ _____

30. $10\frac{3}{4}$ _____

163

8. MULTIPLYING FRACTIONS

Multiply. Simplify the answers.

31. $\frac{2}{5} \times \frac{1}{2} =$ _____

32. $\frac{3}{7} \times \frac{2}{3} =$ _____

33. $\frac{1}{8} \times \frac{2}{5} =$ _____

34. $\frac{7}{9} \times \frac{3}{10} =$ _____

35. $\frac{7}{12} \times \frac{1}{4} =$ _____

Use canceling to reduce to lowest terms.

36. $\frac{35}{45}$ _____

37. $\frac{42}{63}$ _____

38. $\frac{12}{40}$ _____

39. $\frac{27}{81}$ _____

40. $\frac{14}{42}$ _____

Simplify by canceling, then multiply.

41. $\frac{4}{9} \times \frac{9}{36} =$ _____

42. $\frac{25}{32} \times \frac{8}{15} =$ _____

43. $\frac{22}{27} \times \frac{18}{33} =$ _____

44. $\frac{2}{7} \times \frac{49}{50} =$ _____

45. $\frac{7}{35} \times \frac{25}{32} =$ _____

Solve.

46. Mary had 24 tickets to a rap concert. She sold $\frac{1}{4}$ of them. How many tickets did she sell?

_____

47. Rosa mailed 9 boxes, each weighing $\frac{3}{4}$ pound. How much do they weigh altogether?

_____

48. In the last local election in Mike's town, 200 people voted. $\frac{7}{8}$ of the voters were women. How many voters were women?

_____

49. Toshio spent $\frac{1}{3}$ of his money on sports clothes. $\frac{1}{2}$ of that money was spent on shoes. What fraction of his money was spent on shoes?

_____

50. Geraldo spoke for $\frac{5}{6}$ of an hour. $\frac{1}{2}$ of the time he introduced people. What fraction of the hour did he use to make introductions?

_____

51. Smith travels $5\frac{2}{7}$ miles each way to get to work 5 days a week. How far does he travel to work and back each week?

_____

164

9. Dividing Fractions

9.1 Dividing a Whole Number by a Fraction

Dividing a whole number by a fraction is just like multiplying the number by a fraction—with one extra step first. This lesson will show you what that extra step is and will also show you how to complete the division.

Carol works for a phone company. She needs pieces of wire that are $\frac{2}{3}$ yard long to install her equipment. How many pieces can she get from a 6-yard roll of wire?

To solve this problem, divide:

$$6 \div \frac{2}{3} = ?$$

In this example, a whole number is divided by a fraction.

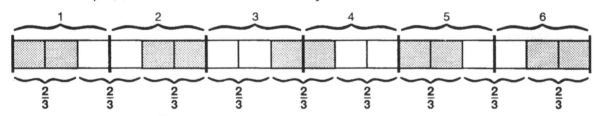

Count the number of $\frac{2}{3}$'s that make up 6—there are 9.

$$6 \div \frac{2}{3} = 9$$

A fast way to divide a whole number by a fraction uses what is called the *reciprocal* of the fraction.

To find the reciprocal, "flip" the fraction—turn it upside down. Exchange the numerator and the denominator.

The reciprocal of $\frac{3}{4}$ is $\frac{4}{3}$. The reciprocal of $\frac{8}{5}$ is $\frac{5}{8}$.

9. DIVIDING FRACTIONS

You can even find the reciprocal of whole numbers.

Since $14 = \frac{14}{1}$, the reciprocal of 14 is $\frac{1}{14}$.

RULE: *How to divide a whole number by a fraction:*

> **1. Write the reciprocal of the fraction you divide by.**
>
> **2. Multiply the whole number by the reciprocal.**

EXAMPLE 1

Divide $10 \div \frac{5}{7}$ = **?**

1. The reciprocal of $\frac{5}{7}$ is $\frac{7}{5}$.

2. Multiply: $\frac{10}{1} \times \frac{7}{5}$ = **?**

3. Simplify by canceling:

$$\frac{\overset{2}{\cancel{10}}}{1} \times \frac{7}{\underset{1}{\cancel{5}}} = \text{?}$$

$$\frac{2}{1} \times \frac{7}{1} = \frac{14}{1} = 14$$

The answer is 14.

EXAMPLE 2

Divide $22 \div 2\frac{1}{2}$ = **?**

In this example, first change the mixed number to a fraction greater than 1:

$$2\frac{1}{2} = \frac{5}{2}$$

1. The reciprocal of $\frac{5}{2}$ is $\frac{2}{5}$.

2. Multiply:

$$22 \times \frac{2}{5} = \frac{44}{5} = 8\frac{4}{5}$$

The answer is $8\frac{4}{5}$.

9.1 DIVIDING A WHOLE NUMBER BY A FRACTION

Exercises with Hints

Write the reciprocals of these fractions.
(Hint: To get the reciprocal, "flip" the fraction.)

1. $\dfrac{4}{9}$ _____

2. $\dfrac{7}{3}$ _____

3. $\dfrac{17}{18}$ _____

4. $\dfrac{6}{13}$ _____

Fill in the missing numbers in the chart.
(Hint: Change mixed numbers to fractions greater than 1. Then find the reciprocal of the fraction.)

	Mixed Number	Fraction Greater Than 1	Reciprocal of Fraction
5.	$3\dfrac{1}{5}$	_____	_____
6.	$7\dfrac{2}{3}$	_____	_____
7.	_____	$\dfrac{9}{4}$	_____
8.	_____	$\dfrac{7}{3}$	_____
9.	_____	_____	$\dfrac{7}{22}$
10.	_____	$\dfrac{31}{4}$	_____

Divide. (Simplify by canceling before you multiply.)
(Hint: Multiply by the <u>reciprocal</u> of the fraction you divide by.)

11. $10 \div \dfrac{5}{6} =$ _____

12. $12 \div \dfrac{2}{3} =$ _____

13. $15 \div 1\dfrac{2}{3} =$ _____

14. $20 \div \dfrac{4}{5} =$ _____

15. $60 \div \dfrac{3}{4} =$ _____

16. $25 \div 4\dfrac{2}{7} =$ _____

17. $30 \div 8 =$ _____

(Hint: Form the reciprocal of a whole number by placing 1 over the whole number.)

Solve.

18. Joan works as a waitress. She has 9 breads and has to place $\dfrac{3}{4}$ of a bread on each table. How many tables will get bread?
(Hint: When you divide by a fraction, you need to find the reciprocal before you multiply.)

_____

167

Exercises on Your Own

Write the missing numbers in the chart.

Mixed Number	Fraction Greater Than 1	Reciprocal of Fraction
1. $4\frac{3}{4}$	_____	_____
2. $10\frac{2}{3}$	_____	_____
3. _____	$\frac{7}{2}$	_____
4. _____	$\frac{17}{6}$	_____
5. _____	_____	$\frac{3}{16}$
6. _____	$\frac{40}{7}$	_____

Divide. (If you can, simplify by canceling before you multiply.)

7. $12 \div \frac{2}{3} =$ _____

8. $7 \div \frac{4}{5} =$ _____

9. $5 \div \frac{7}{8} =$ _____

10. $24 \div \frac{6}{7} =$ _____

11. $18 \div 2\frac{1}{6} =$ _____

12. $3 \div 5\frac{1}{2} =$ _____

13. $15 \div 25 =$ _____

Solve.

14. Bart needs to interview a number of people. Each interview will take $\frac{2}{5}$ hour. How many people can he interview in 6 hours?

_____

15. Jina has 9 feet of packaging tape to wrap boxes. Each box takes $\frac{3}{4}$ foot. How many boxes can Jina wrap?

_____

9.2 Dividing a Fraction by Fraction or a Whole Number

This lesson will give you more practice in working division problems that contain fractions. As you learned in the last lesson, the first step is to change the number you divide by into its reciprocal. If you've forgotten what a reciprocal is, this lesson will remind you.

Dolly wants to serve pieces of pizza that are $\frac{1}{6}$ of a pie each. How many servings can she get from $\frac{2}{3}$ of a pie?

To find the answer, divide:

$$\frac{2}{3} \div \frac{1}{6} = ?$$

How many $\frac{1}{6}$ pieces are in $\frac{2}{3}$?

Here is a drawing that can help.

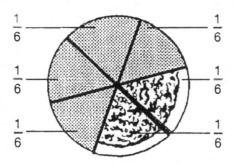

There are four $\frac{1}{6}$ pieces in $\frac{2}{3}$ of a pizza.

Dolly can get four servings from $\frac{2}{3}$ of a pizza.

As you learned in the last lesson, a fast way to divide a number by a fraction uses the **reciprocal**.

To find the reciprocal, "flip" the fraction—exchange the numerator and the denominator.

For example, the reciprocal of $\frac{4}{7}$ is $\frac{7}{4}$.

And the reciprocal of $\frac{3}{10}$ is $\frac{10}{3}$.

And since $8 = \frac{8}{1}$, the reciprocal of 8 is $\frac{1}{8}$.

9. DIVIDING FRACTIONS

RULE: *How to divide a fraction by another fraction:*

1. *Write the reciprocal of the number you divide by—in this case, the second fraction.*

2. *Multiply the first fraction by this reciprocal. Cancel if you can before multiplying.*

EXAMPLE 1

Divide: $\dfrac{4}{5} \div \dfrac{3}{10} = ?$

1. Write the reciprocal of the number you divide by:

   The reciprocal of $\dfrac{3}{10}$ is $\dfrac{10}{3}$.

2. Multiply the first fraction by this reciprocal.

   $$\dfrac{4}{5} \times \dfrac{10}{3} = ?$$

   Cancel:

   $$\dfrac{4}{\cancel{5}_{1}} \times \dfrac{\overset{2}{\cancel{10}}}{3} = \dfrac{8}{3}$$

   Write the answer as a mixed number: $\dfrac{8}{3} = 2\dfrac{2}{3}$

EXAMPLE 2

Divide: $\dfrac{5}{9} \div \dfrac{2}{3} = ?$

1. Write the reciprocal of the number you divide by:

   The reciprocal of $\dfrac{2}{3}$ is $\dfrac{3}{2}$.

2. Multiply the first fraction by this reciprocal.

   $$\dfrac{5}{9} \times \dfrac{3}{2} = ?$$

   Cancel:

   $$\dfrac{5}{\cancel{9}_{3}} \times \dfrac{\overset{1}{\cancel{3}}}{2} = \dfrac{5}{6}$$

170

9.2 DIVIDING A FRACTION BY A FRACTION OR A WHOLE NUMBER

EXAMPLE 3

Divide: $\dfrac{7}{11} \div 14 = ?$

This is an example of a fraction divided by a whole number.

1. Write the reciprocal of the number you divide by:

   The reciprocal of 14 is $\dfrac{1}{14}$.

2. Multiply the first fraction by this reciprocal.

$$\frac{7}{11} \times \frac{1}{14} = ?$$

Cancel:

$$\frac{\overset{1}{\cancel{7}}}{11} \times \frac{1}{\underset{2}{\cancel{14}}} = \frac{1}{22}$$

Exercises with Hints

Write the reciprocal of each fraction.
*(Hint: Remember, to get the reciprocal,
"flip" the fraction.)*

1. $\dfrac{5}{8}$ _____

2. $\dfrac{13}{20}$ _____

3. $\dfrac{5}{2}$ _____

4. $\dfrac{25}{32}$ _____

Write the reciprocal of each whole
number.
*(Hint: Form the reciprocal of a whole
number by placing 1 over the whole
number.)*

5. 7 _____

6. 20 _____

7. 95 _____

8. 127 _____

Divide.
*(Hint: Don't forget to write the reciprocal
of the second number—the number you
divide by. Then multiply.)*

9. $\dfrac{7}{8} \div \dfrac{5}{4} =$ _____

10. $\dfrac{7}{10} \div \dfrac{21}{25} =$ _____

11. $\dfrac{5}{8} \div \dfrac{1}{2} =$ _____

9. DIVIDING FRACTIONS

Solve.

(Hint: When you divide by a fraction, you need to find the reciprocal before you multiply.)

12. Harriet has $\frac{3}{4}$ gallons of orange juice. She has to give $\frac{1}{8}$ gallon of juice to each group. How many groups will get juice?

_____

13. For the first $\frac{2}{3}$ mile of the race, there was a person posted at every $\frac{1}{9}$ of a mile. How many people were posted over the first $\frac{2}{3}$ mile?

_____

Exercises on Your Own

Write the reciprocal of each number.

1. $\frac{7}{11}$ _____

2. 56 _____

3. $\frac{13}{5}$ _____

4. 121 _____

Reduce the fraction to the simplest fraction by canceling.

5. $\frac{45}{60}$ _____

6. $\frac{7}{49}$ _____

7. $\frac{18}{56}$ _____

8. $\frac{22}{99}$ _____

Divide. (Cancel before multiplying.)

9. $\frac{9}{14} \div \frac{3}{4} =$ _____

10. $\frac{24}{25} \div \frac{72}{85} =$ _____

11. $\frac{9}{30} \div \frac{18}{25} =$ _____

12. $\frac{9}{10} \div \frac{81}{100} =$ _____

Solve.

13. Kenny has $\frac{4}{5}$ of a can of paint. He gives each child $\frac{1}{10}$ of a can of paint. How many children can he give paint to?

_____

14. Dennis tuned the radio on and listened for $\frac{3}{5}$ hour. After he turned it on, he heard a commercial every $\frac{1}{10}$ of an hour. How many commercials did he hear?

_____

15. Evelyn decided to take $\frac{2}{3}$ of her fortune and divide it among her dearest friends. Each friend got $\frac{1}{6}$ of this part of her fortune. How many friends does she have?

_____

172

9.3 Dividing by a Mixed Number

This is the last lesson in division—and the last lesson in the book. You will learn how to divide mixed numbers. As you will see, all you have to do is change the mixed numbers into fractions greater than 1, and then divide in the usual way.

Sonny wants to decorate some flagpoles with ribbons. He has $19\frac{1}{4}$ yards of ribbon.

For each flagpole, he needs $1\frac{1}{6}$ yards of ribbon.

How many flagpoles can he decorate?

To find the solution, divide. How many $1\frac{1}{6}$'s in $19\frac{1}{4}$?

$$19\frac{1}{4} \div 1\frac{1}{6} = ?$$

This problem shows a mixed number divided by a mixed number.

You can find the answer by adapting the same method as in the other lessons in this chapter.

RULE: *How to divide by a mixed number:*

1. *Write mixed numbers as improper fractions.*
2. *Write the reciprocal of the second number (the number you divide by).*
3. *Multiply the first number by the reciprocal of the second number.*

9. DIVIDING FRACTIONS

Using these three steps on the problem at the beginning of this lesson:

$$19\frac{1}{4} \div 1\frac{1}{6} = \;?$$

1. Write the mixed numbers as fractions greater than 1:

$$\frac{77}{4} \div \frac{7}{6} = \;?$$

2. Write the reciprocal of the number you divide by:

The reciprocal of $\frac{7}{6}$ is $\frac{6}{7}$.

3. Multiply the first fraction by this reciprocal.

$$\frac{77}{4} \times \frac{6}{7} = \;?$$

Cancel:

$$\frac{\overset{11}{\cancel{77}}}{\underset{2}{\cancel{4}}} \times \frac{\overset{3}{\cancel{6}}}{\underset{1}{\cancel{7}}} = \frac{33}{2} = 16\frac{1}{2}$$

Sonny can decorate 16 flagpoles. He doesn't have enough for 17 flagpoles.

EXAMPLE 1

$$5\frac{3}{5} \div 1\frac{1}{6} = \;?$$

  1. Write mixed numbers as fractions greater than 1.

$$\frac{28}{5} \div \frac{7}{6} = \;?$$

  2. Write the reciprocal of the number you divide by:

The reciprocal of $\frac{7}{6}$ is $\frac{6}{7}$.

  3. Multiply the first fraction by this reciprocal:

$$\frac{28}{5} \times \frac{6}{7} = \;?$$

Cancel:

$$\frac{\overset{4}{\cancel{28}}}{5} \times \frac{6}{\underset{1}{\cancel{7}}} = \frac{24}{5} = 4\frac{4}{5}$$

174

9.3 DIVIDING BY A MIXED NUMBER

EXAMPLE 2

$$\frac{5}{12} \div 3\frac{3}{4} = ?$$

1. Write mixed numbers as fractions greater than 1.

$$\frac{5}{12} \div \frac{15}{4} = ?$$

2. Write the reciprocal of the number you divide by:

The reciprocal of $\frac{15}{4}$ is $\frac{4}{15}$.

3. Multiply the first fraction by this reciprocal:

$$\frac{5}{12} \times \frac{4}{15} = ?$$

Cancel:

$$\frac{\overset{1}{\cancel{5}}}{\underset{3}{\cancel{12}}} \times \frac{\overset{1}{\cancel{4}}}{\underset{3}{\cancel{15}}} = \frac{1}{9}$$

Exercises with Hints

Put a check mark before each fraction greater than 1.
(Hint: Remember that the numerator of a fraction greater than 1 is greater than the denominator.)

1. ☐ $\frac{2}{3}$

2. ☐ $\frac{7}{6}$

3. ☐ $\frac{14}{3}$

4. ☐ $\frac{10}{10}$

Write each mixed number as a fraction greater than 1.
(Hint: Multiply the denominator by the whole number, then add the numerator.)

5. $4\frac{1}{7}$ _____

6. $10\frac{3}{8}$ _____

7. $25\frac{1}{2}$ _____

8. $100\frac{4}{7}$ _____

175

9. DIVIDING FRACTIONS

Write the reciprocal of these numbers.
(Hint: To find the reciprocal of a number,
flip the fraction—exchange the numerator
and the denominator.)

9. 45 _____

10. $\frac{4}{23}$ _____

11. $\frac{8}{11}$ _____

12. 9 _____

Divide. (Cancel before multiplying.)
(Hint: Don't forget to write the second
number as a reciprocal.)

13. $\frac{2}{3} \div 1\frac{1}{3} =$ _____

14. $4\frac{4}{9} \div \frac{20}{27} =$ _____

15. $3\frac{1}{2} \div 1\frac{1}{4} =$ _____

16. $20 \div 4\frac{4}{9} =$ _____

Solve.
(Hint: First, decide which number you
divide by, then write its reciprocal.)

17. George has 18 vitamin pills left.
He takes one and a half vitamin pills
a day. How long will his pills last?

_____

18. Clarence spoke several times for a
total of $2\frac{1}{2}$ hours. He spoke for
$\frac{1}{2}$ hour each time. How many different times did he speak?

_____

Exercises on Your Own

Write the mixed numbers as improper
fractions:

1. $4\frac{5}{8}$ _____

2. $3\frac{7}{9}$ _____

3. $12\frac{1}{7}$ _____

4. $5\frac{3}{10}$ _____

Write the reciprocal of each number.

5. $\frac{4}{5}$ _____

6. 83 _____

7. $\frac{45}{3}$ _____

8. $\frac{11}{12}$ _____

9.3 DIVIDING BY A MIXED NUMBER

Divide. (Cancel before multiplying.)

9. $\dfrac{4}{7} \div \dfrac{16}{28} =$ _____

10. $2\dfrac{4}{5} \div \dfrac{7}{8} =$ _____

11. $9\dfrac{3}{8} \div 12\dfrac{1}{2} =$ _____

12. $7\dfrac{1}{2} \div \dfrac{5}{6} =$ _____

13. $\dfrac{4}{5} \div 5\dfrac{1}{7} =$ _____

14. $5\dfrac{2}{15} \div 8\dfrac{2}{5} =$ _____

Solve.

15. Lillian wants to make a neat chart in her report. She made her chart $6\dfrac{3}{4}$ inches wide, with each column $1\dfrac{1}{8}$ inches wide. How many columns will she have?

_____

16. Franz studies music, and is trying to figure out how many eighth ($\dfrac{1}{8}$) notes are in a half ($\dfrac{1}{2}$) note. How many are there?

_____

17. The shelf in Joe's office has only $20\dfrac{1}{4}$ inches for books. He ordered a series of books on tax law, each of which is $2\dfrac{1}{4}$ inches wide. How many books can fit on the shelf?

_____

177

9.4 Review

Write the reciprocal of each number.

1. $\dfrac{4}{5}$ _____

2. $\dfrac{7}{11}$ _____

3. 14 _____

Write the missing numbers in the chart.

Mixed Number	Fraction > 1	Reciprocal of Fraction > 1
4. $7\dfrac{1}{2}$	_____	_____
5. _____	$\dfrac{12}{5}$	_____
6. _____		$\dfrac{2}{7}$
7. _____	$\dfrac{15}{2}$	_____
8. $10\dfrac{2}{5}$	_____	_____

Divide.
(If you can, simplify before you multiply.)

9. $9 \div \dfrac{3}{4} =$ _____

10. $10 \div \dfrac{3}{5} =$ _____

11. $80 \div \dfrac{20}{21} =$ _____

Divide.
(Cancel before multiplying.)

12. $\dfrac{2}{3} \div \dfrac{5}{6} =$ _____

13. $\dfrac{7}{8} \div \dfrac{3}{4} =$ _____

14. $\dfrac{7}{12} \div \dfrac{14}{21} =$ _____

15. $\dfrac{4}{15} \div \dfrac{16}{25} =$ _____

16. $\dfrac{27}{30} \div \dfrac{9}{10} =$ _____

Divide with mixed numbers.
(Cancel before multiplying.)

17. $3\dfrac{3}{4} \div \dfrac{5}{6} =$ _____

18. $2\dfrac{5}{8} \div 1\dfrac{3}{4} =$ _____

19. $8\dfrac{2}{5} \div 5\dfrac{1}{4} =$ _____

20. $6\dfrac{2}{9} \div 9\dfrac{1}{3} =$ _____

21. $1\dfrac{1}{2} \div \dfrac{5}{16} =$ _____